Lovers in the Wilderness

Lovers in the Wilderness

Awaken Mystical Unity and Create a Joyful Life with Mantra Prayer

STEPHANIE RUTT

Foreword by Robert A. Jonas

RESOURCE *Publications* • Eugene, Oregon

LOVERS IN THE WILDERNESS
Awaken Mystical Unity and Create a Joyful Life with Mantra Prayer

Copyright © 2021 Stephanie Rutt. All rights reserved. Except for brief quotations in critical publications or reviews, no part of this book may be reproduced in any manner without prior written permission from the publisher. Write: Permissions, Wipf and Stock Publishers, 199 W. 8th Ave., Suite 3, Eugene, OR 97401.

Resource Publications
An Imprint of Wipf and Stock Publishers
199 W. 8th Ave., Suite 3
Eugene, OR 97401

www.wipfandstock.com

PAPERBACK ISBN: 978-1-7252-6641-4
HARDCOVER ISBN: 978-1-7252-6642-1
EBOOK ISBN: 978-1-7252-6643-8

01/11/21

For all those who brave the wilderness

Contents

Foreword by Robert A. Jonas	ix
Preface	xi
Acknowledgments	xiii
Introduction: The Search for Mystical Unity	xv

PART 1: BECOMING LOVERS

1	Answering the Call	3
2	Leaving the Trail	7
3	Preparing a Space	11

PART 2: BRAVING THE WILDERNESS

4	Getting Tuned	17
5	Walking in Harmony	24
6	Merging Will and Surrender	37

PART 3: SINGING THE HOLY

7	Preparing Your Spiritual Practice Crucible	45
8	Creating a Mantra Prayer Practice	51
9	Navigating through Obstacles	57

Contents

Conclusion: What Lovers Know	67
Appendix A: Sample Mantra Prayers from Six Faith Traditions	73
Appendix B: Stories from Lovers Who Have Braved the Wilderness	106
Bibliography	119

Foreword

YEARS AGO, I VISITED Stephanie's Tree of Life community and saw firsthand the loving attention and respect with which she greeted participants, listening with great interest to their stories and listening, above all, for the heartbeat of new life. I soon realized that anyone who participates in one of Stephanie's events is greeted as a friend. She embodies the magnificent message that she conveys in her many blog posts and books: each of us can manifest the Light of divinity in our daily lives, even in the midst of our worries and pains.

Lovers in the Wilderness is rich with nourishment for the soul and for communities that feel drawn to the practice of Mantra Prayer. Stephanie's spiritual vision is vitally needed, especially now, when democracies worldwide are threatened by the rise of autocracies riven with hate, when our natural world is being plundered and desecrated, when America's legacy of slavery and white supremacy is being laid bare, and when truth itself is on trial. Our country needs better laws and policies, honest politicians dedicated to the common good, and peaceful political action and protest when laws and practices are unjust—indeed, we need to transform society at every level in order to build a more just, safe, and habitable world. But in order to do this, we will also need spiritual transformation, a rekindling of the love that connects us to each other and to the rest of life. Stephanie offers a pathway to a revolutionary love, one that transcends our habits of self-rejection, anxiety, worry, and anger, a pathway that can renew our world.

Following the path of Mantra Prayer requires dedication and discipline, but the rewards are great. I expect that Stephanie would agree with the medieval Dominican friar Meister Eckhart, who wrote that we are called not merely to love each other nor merely to carry out just behaviors for moral reasons; rather, we are called to *be* love and to *be* justice in all that we do. Mantra Prayer isn't simply a moral or ethical path; it can't be attained simply by offering our external obedience or by following certain prescribed steps. Rather, this is a path that works from the inside out, setting us free to become a manifestation or embodiment of divine love.

The reader will appreciate Stephanie's brilliant and yet unpretentious mining of all the world's ancient spiritual traditions. Like a bee, she draws wisdom from the flowers of Judaism, Christianity, Sufism, Hinduism, Buddhism, and Sikhism. She knows that the wisdom she shares is not hers alone, nor possessed by any single spiritual tradition. Properly understood, her inter-spiritual journey reveals what countless philosophers and spiritual teachers—such as Aldous Huxley in his great work *The Perennial Tradition*—have discovered: namely, that truth, beauty, goodness, and love are universal, eternal qualities that we can realize in our own lives.

Anyone who longs to discover their true self and inner wisdom, and anyone who is willing to get serious about his or her spiritual growth, will eagerly partake of the banquet that Stephanie has set before us.

—Dr. Robert A. Jonas, a biographer of Henri Nouwen, and author of *Rebecca: A Father's Journey from Grief to Gratitude*. Dr. Jonas is an environmental activist and founder of The Empty Bell sanctuary, a contemplative center for Christian–Buddhist dialogue (emptybell.org) in western Massachusetts.

Preface

I AM A LOVER. A lover of God—the one called by many names—the one to whom we can only point, for the minute we say a thing, try to describe the indescribable, we fall short! And, over many years, I've trudged through my own inner wilderness, dragging along my ball-and-chain resistance, praying for the courage to enter those dark caves of my deepest fears, hurts, and anger. But, once I started, I found there was no choice but to continue if I wanted to be free, free of that ball and chain. More than anything, I just wanted to know peace.

The journey, of course, continues, but I travel a bit lighter these days because, along the way, I've been brought to my knees more than once—and more than once have been saved by Mantra Prayer, but, perhaps, not in the way you might think. Mantra Prayer has brought me to love, the deepest love I've ever known, a love that has left me more often in ways I could have never foreseen or imagined, fully surrendered in the soft hand of God. Working with Mantra Prayer has taught me how to create the conditions to invite mystical unity with God and, as a result, to know the joy that does, indeed, come in the morning (see Ps 30:5). I call moments of mystical unity gifts of grace as they come in their own time and way. And, in those precious moments of unity, I've wondrously discovered that all those agonizing times spent in those dark caves, the very ones I so adamantly resisted for so long, were, indeed, a small price to pay for what I've received.

So, it's with a humble heart that I offer this book to all those wanting to explore the inner wilderness and learn how to create the conditions for mystical unity and to, ultimately, experience a new sense of joy—an internal joy not predicated on outer circumstances. My hope is that the timely release of this book, in the middle of the COVID-19 pandemic, may, in particular, help all those who are struggling to remember what is possible and to provide some concrete tools to discover that internal joy—that still point within. This place awakens the eternal mystery already there waiting in the silence and allows the seeker to know that it's still possible to create a life of joy and beauty even as all seems to be spinning, ravaging, out of control.

But disclaimer! You, too, may just discover that love beyond all understanding and, as a result, find yourself to be, above and beyond all else, a lover.

And, if so, rest assured, nothing will be the same.

Acknowledgments

We don't journey alone. I couldn't be writing this book without all those in my beloved Tree of Life interfaith community, many with whom I've long journeyed, to bring forth our amazing vision of interfaith and to begin to redefine and reimagine church. For many years, we have studied, shared, and grown together in many sacred circles. Though I've had the role of founder, leader, and teacher, I've received infinite and continued blessings and have learned so very much from each and every person in our community. In many ways, we've written this book together. Thank you.

For almost thirty years I've immersed myself in the spiritual practices across faith traditions and along the way have sought the guidance of many skilled and gifted teachers. I have always felt it important to acknowledge the shoulders upon which we stand, those who have come before us and, in particular, those who have helped us along the way. Some teachers have, indeed, supported me in crucial ways. Others have challenged me in unexpected ways. Yet, all have contributed to my spiritual growth and, therefore, to the recording of the journey found in this book. Thank you.

And to my dear husband who's always supported my work, who's read every blog, every chapter of every book before publishing, for his wonderful, clear, helpful thoughts and insights. Knowing me so well, he often knows what I'm wanting to say but, at times, may just be missing the mark. Thank you.

And, finally, I'd like to acknowledge Dr. Robert A. Jonas, for his time and care in contributing the foreword and, also, Rev. Laurie Van Dyck for her very helpful proofreading and editing skills. Each has blessed this book in unique ways. Thank you.

> No one escapes the wilderness on the way to the promised land.
>
> —Annie Dillard

INTRODUCTION

The Search for Mystical Unity

MYSTICAL UNITY. POETS DREAM about it. Scholars analyzed it. Saints and Avatars across faith traditions have lived it. And, throughout time, ordinary seekers, like you and me, have yearned for it. It's why we pray, meditate, sing, and chant. It's why we rise early for morning prayers, hold fast to familiar ritual, seek wisdom from religious and spiritual leaders. In particular, it's what we cry out for when life circumstances have brought us to the end of all we know and we're left feeling lost, alone, and adrift on a dark, unforgiving sea. We sense, at such times, that some, any, connection with the great divine is all that can save us. Now, it's all that matters. And it's our very yearning for such connection that can also kindle hope that perhaps, just perhaps, joy may, can, *will* come in the morning (see Ps 30:5). Just the imagining can spark a weary heart to mourn for its life again.

Still, while we recognize this ubiquitous yearning for mystical unity with that-which-is-beyond-understanding across the human spectrum, and can find it heralded as the pinnacle of religious experience, it's perhaps the most difficult of all experiences to describe. Simply, it can be. Yet, many who've brought their yearning hearts to prayer, in multiple ways across faith traditions, know this place well, this place that resides just beyond our understanding. They know because they've been touched—touched by an indescribable, yet unmistakable, experience. They've been blessed to hear, to sense, to *know* the holy one in a truly visceral way. And as a result, a fundamental shift happens. Now, they find that they trust this place, this place just beyond understanding, more—infinitely more—than anything known before.

And, sometimes, most blessedly, perhaps the purest form of mystical unity may occur—moments of full emersion with our beloved God that dissolve all separations and distinctions. Blessedly, such moments are only recognizable in hindsight as, graciously and quite unexpectedly, we are brought outside the finite realm of time and space and into the infinite, eternal heart of God. And here . . . we are left humbled, still, and filled with awe.

Such sweet moments of unity leave us, in particular, fully aware of Kabir's revelation: "All know that the drop merges into the ocean but few know that the ocean merges into the drop."[1] For in moments of mystical unity, we as a drop in the ocean of God experience being the omnipresence known only to the ocean. It's not an experience of ourselves as a small, tiny part, suddenly feeling like a part of the whole. No. In fact, it's not a feeling at all, or a thought for that matter. It's the experience of *being* the ocean itself. Now that greatest of all fears echoed across faith traditions—that we're separate and alone—is fully negated by the experience of mystical unity. We know now we could never be alone. We know now as Jesus knew, "I and the Father are one" (John 10:30).

I'm fond of calling all moments of mystical unity love's kiss because, in truth, they make lovers out of us and send us out again and again into our inner wilderness in search of that love everlasting that now we know is real. Such is the gift of Mantra Prayer, which, through its sacred sound current, helps us to create those conditions for mystical unity deep in the depths of the silence that follows our prayers.

And, most graciously, such experiences linger close like a sweet fragrance that, with just the remembrance, can rekindle something akin to joy—that eternal devotional joy fully capable of sustaining us through all weather patterns particularly when, suddenly, we find ourselves alone and adrift on that unforgiving sea. For even then, we find we can conjure up an inner smile knowing now as the

---

1. Kabir, *Bijak*, 96.

The Search for Mystical Unity

Paramahansa Yogananda knew, "From joy I came, for joy I live, in sacred joy I melt."[2] We know now because we've been kissed.

And, once kissed, the yearning for more becomes insatiable. With parched lips, we journey through our inner wilderness in search of that fountain, that kiss, again and again. Along the way, we're brought to our knees and left empty and aching, filled with nothing but that yearning. And we're raised up to soar with eagles on states of grace we could have never believed, imagined, or known were possible. Just the memory of the kiss propels us forward. It is both deeply personal and, yet, not personal at all, for now that we've been touched by the indescribable, we can find delight in being a unique expression of the creator, a single drop in the ocean, and, at the same time, we know we are one with all. We've been the ocean. We've glimpsed eternity. We've been kissed.

In this book, I'll show you how to journey through your own inner wilderness and, using Mantra Prayer, create the conditions to invite love's kiss, experience moments of mystical unity with the holy one, and to, as a result, create a life of joy. We'll begin in Part 1, "Becoming Lovers," exploring the essential preparations for the journey. Here we'll examine how lovers are called in chapter 1, "Answering the Call," reflect upon the importance of changing out the known for the unknown in chapter 2, "Leaving the Trail," and contemplate where to find the mystery that awaits in chapter 3, "Preparing a Space."

In Part 2, "Braving the Wilderness," we'll discuss what I call the love embedded in the sound current of sacred practices in chapter 4, "Getting Tuned," and how to engage that love to create the conditions for mystical unity with the beloved, God, in the silence that follows. Here we'll explore the paradigm I first introduced in *The Call of the Mourning Dove: How Sacred Sound Awakens Mystical Unity*, the Sonic Trilogy of Love. In chapter 5, "Walking in Harmony," we'll consider valuable guidelines for working with Mantra Prayer and, in chapter 6, "Merging Will and Surrender," explore the intersection of personal will and divine surrender critical to creating those conditions for mystical unity and moments of joy.

2. Radhakrishnan, *Principal Upanisads*, 557.

In Part 3, "Singing the Holy," you'll prepare for this inner wilderness journey with key guidelines in chapter 7, "Preparing Your Spiritual Practice Crucible," be guided through a detailed process for designing a practice in chapter 8, "Creating a Mantra Prayer Practice," and be shown how to work with the resistance that arises in chapter 9, "Navigating through Obstacles." Finally, in the conclusion, "What Lovers Know," you'll explore what you need to know to keep your heart open to moments of mystical unity in daily life.

Finally, in Appendix A, you're offered a sampling of Mantra Prayers from six faith traditions: Judaism, Christianity, Sufism, Hinduism, Buddhism, and Sikhism. These practices have been chosen for their particular resonance for cultivating healing and forgiveness, courage and focus, and abundance. And in Appendix B, you'll enjoy hearing stories from other lovers who have braved the wilderness to awaken mystical unity and create a joyful life with Mantra Prayer.

Become a lover.

Brave the wilderness.

Sing the holy...

And be cracked open and set free.

Part 1

Becoming Lovers

1

Answering the Call

Let us be silent that we may hear the whispers of God.[1]

RALPH WALDO EMERSON

TO BECOME LOVERS, WE must answer the call, leave the trail, and prepare a space. Each of these important steps are explored here in Part 1, "Becoming Lovers."

All lovers are called. And we're all lovers. Yet, some hear and heed the call and others do not. The call invites us to exit off the known way to enter into the inner wilderness where conditions may be set to welcome the mystery, unforeseen moments of mystical unity with our God. The call is often described as a whisper, for it requires us to become very still and quiet so as to hear. "Be still and know that I am God," the Psalmist tells us (Ps 46:10). How extraordinary to know that God is always near, whispering in our inner silence, ready to guide us through our most challenging and terrifying times; smiling with us in those times of unencumbered bliss. Yet, sometimes, we may recognize the whisper only in hindsight as having tried to reach us through our intuition, though we chose not to hear it. It's in those times we may cry out, "I knew but . . . !"

---

1. Emerson, "Natural History," 19.

Part 1: Becoming Lovers

The call. We can ignore it. Deny it. Make believe we didn't hear. Walk away from it. Our choice. But that relentless call, whisper, will persevere. Why? Ah, the answer may surprise you. It's because, in truth, our blessed creator longs for us as much as we could ever long for him. Sufis call this *Ya Tawwab*, one of the beautiful ninety-nine names of Allah, where we discover that, when we turn away from our perceived fault and toward Allah, we find Allah looking at us with endless compassion.[2]

Just imagine. All those times, in response to some difficult life-altering experience, accident, unforeseen diagnosis, unexpected tragedy to ourselves or a loved one, times that can leave us feeling alone and adrift on that unforgiving sea, we may have cried out, "Okay, God! Where the h*ll are you?!" God had actually been there patiently yearning for us, whispering to our hearts, all the while, all along. It was we who couldn't hear.

This is such an important awareness because, while we're certainly not promised a problem-free life, we are promised that we could never be alone. In Psalm 23, we're assured of this in the first line. Normally this line is translated, "The Lord is my Shepherd. I shall not want." But in Hebrew the translation is a bit different. The "I shall not want" is expressed as *Lo Echsar*, which actually translates, "I lack not."[3] Important! This reminds us that even when it feels like all of life is falling apart around us, it's possible to remember *Lo Echsar*, to experience ourselves as already full—as lacking nothing—to remember that we are not alone. Such a remembrance can be like a beacon from a lighthouse guiding us safely across that unforgiving sea.

In addition to the whisper coming in response to hardship, it can also come amplified in moments of unexpected bliss to suddenly jolt us awake from a sleep when we didn't even know we were dreaming. Like playing peek-a-boo, God surprises us, purposefully catching us off guard, so we can see, feel, know what is—has always been—right before us. Like the day I nervously sat at the stoplight watching a homeless man come closer and closer, until he was

---

2. Meyer et al., *Physicians of the Heart*, 67.
3. Scherman et al., *Tehillim*, 56.

standing by my door and our eyes met and I . . . *saw* him. Without thinking, I reached in my wallet and handed him a five-dollar bill. He thanked me kindly, the light changed, and off I went.

And all these years later he's still with me. And what an uneven exchange! He only got a five-dollar bill. I got a glimpse of the eternal. "The eye with which I see God is the same eye with which God sees me," Meister Eckhart said.[4] Amen.

And sometimes the whisper can guide us where we most certainly wouldn't dare, or want, to go. When a loved one committed suicide and I was thrown into the depths of despair, I discovered that, mostly, my sadness wasn't the problem but my resistance was. The whisper seemed to say, "Follow me," and I was led straight off the deep end to be fully submerged. As I moved through my days, I found myself in some boundaryless state, with no edges, yet feeling alive in a way I hadn't known before. Yes, alive. A veil had come down and there was God. In that bottomless, dark abyss, I'd found only the soft hand of God waiting to catch my endless fall. Love's kiss, indeed.

Whether the circumstances are deeply challenging, serenely blissful, or sorrowful, the whisper, calling to us, will, in time, guide us to experience *all* of our humanity, making it possible for us to walk out like shepherds to see and be seen with God's one eye. It's how all the great ones from the Buddha to Mother Teresa walked straight into the world's suffering to bring a light of hope. It's how we too, you and me, can get up each morning and, listening for that whisper, be guided to be God's eyes, hands, and feet in the world.

Yet, becoming a lover is not for the faint-hearted, for the inner wilderness is formidable. It will strip you down and force you to examine all you've cherished, believed, hoped, dreamed. And, alongside, your deepest fears will be your constant companion, lurking and pacing just waiting for a weak moment. Yes, rest assured, you'll be tested beyond what you may feel you can endure.

Yet, becoming a lover is the only thing that can make you sane, indeed, a bit wild. For just beyond what you've feared most, just that step beyond where you would have rather given up, lies freedom.

---

4. McGinn, *Mystical Thought*, 149.

Part 1: Becoming Lovers

Freedom from being lost to being found as the great hymn "Amazing Grace" proclaimed. Freedom from the illusion of separateness, of believing you are alone. Freedom from being harnessed and tamed by outside influences to becoming guided by your own inner compass.

And how do lovers discover that inner compass? By answering the call and listening deeply for the whisper, always speaking within God's true language: silence. The whisper that's always speaking to our inner ear and quaking heart. It's all that can guide us past the mirage we've been chasing and lead us to the fountain of true everlasting joy where our deepest thirst can finally be satisfied.

Listen in the silence. It's where the whisper speaks. Answer its call. Follow, and know that in any moment, most especially when you're least expecting, love's kiss will find you and make a lover out of you.

2

Leaving the Trail

"Come to the edge," he said. "We're afraid!" they said. "Come to the edge," he said. "But, we're afraid," they said. And he pushed them and they flew.[1]

CHRISTOPHER LOGUE

REST ASSURED THAT WHEN we answer the call and follow where the whispers lead, we'll be led into unfamiliar territory. And, funny thing about stepping off the known way: most of us don't want to go there. As bad as the status quo is, at least it's familiar. Yet, I've discovered, more times than I care to admit, that stepping off the trail into the unknown, making myself blast through fear, anger, and doubt, has brought me some of the most profound gifts of my life. In fact, I've come to know that the greater my belligerence, my full blown "I can't!" or "Not going to happen!" angst, the greater the gift that waits, in equal measure, just on the other side of my resistance.

Such was a time when my Hebrew teacher planted a seed of a whisper in me—one I definitely was not happy about! But, something in me knew she was leading me deeper into my inner wilderness even though I was not at all inclined to follow. I'd sought her

---

1. Apollinaire, Guillaume, "HD Quotes," page 1.

Part 1: Becoming Lovers

out to learn Hebrew so I could recite and translate some of the most beloved psalms, in particular Psalm 23. I had been practicing a particular version of the psalm which was sung and was very melodic and extraordinarily beautiful. I simply loved it. But, one day to my great surprise, my teacher suggested I take on a different practice, Genesis 1, and listen to a recording offered by a well-respected rabbi. She was wanting me to dip deeper into the essence of Hebrew.

I was not happy! What? Put aside my beloved practice? But I've learned to follow the guidance of excellent teachers and so I began. Genesis 1: "In the beginning God created the heavens and the earth."

bə·rê·šîṯ bā·rā 'ĕ·lō·hîm; 'êṯ haš·šā·ma·yim wə·'êṯ hā·'ā·reṣ.[2]

It was not melodic. It was not beautiful. The rabbi's voice seemed quite unpleasant. But every morning I got up, put on my headphones, and began reciting with him, over and over. Then, as always, I'd sit in silence. Still, even then, most of the time I was completely irritated as my mind continued to wonder about complaining.

Then, one morning about three weeks in, as I sat in silence, my mind must have rested just long enough because something happened. The only way I've been able to describe it was that it was like a shutter opened and then closed. Half a second. But it left me stunned and still. I had been given a taste of that love's kiss—a moment in the eternal, a glimpse of eternity, a taste of mystical unity with that which had been silently waiting just beyond all my resistance and my complaining mind. Such is the power of mantra! Even when the mind is clearly lost in distraction, the power of the sacred sound current can still cut through if we persevere.

Over the years, I've had other such moments, unpredictable, sweet moments occurring in regular practice in that silence that follows which have revealed the part of me, of all of us, which was never born and never dies—moments when the ocean of God merges with us as a drop. And again, we recognize them only in hindsight, as they occur in the eternal outside the realm of time and space. They leave us humble, still, and fully knowing that we

---

2. "Genesis 1 Hebrew."

are much more than what we think, feel, or sense. And, most graciously, we begin to understand that the same eternal place in all of us is exactly what unites us beyond all differences. Jesus told us that the kingdom of heaven is within (see Luke 17:21). Krishna in the Bhagavad Gita told us that deep in the hearts of all lies the light of all lights forever beyond darkness (see Sloka 13:17).[3] And it's why the Buddha told us that if we truly loved our self we could never hurt another.[4] Why? Because, at the core of our being, we are the other! What I do to another truly returns to me in equal measure *and* ripples out to impact the entire ocean.

Still, whether you're new to spiritual practice in general or to mantra practice in particular or have been practicing for some time, there are any number of reasons that can cause some trepidation just thinking about facing the wilds of the inner landscape. Some part of us knows that we must journey through territory we may have become quite adept at avoiding. Territory that will invite us to heal our deepest wounds, transform unhelpful core beliefs, sit with new awareness of our part in the creation of our suffering.

Yet, the inner landscape is the only place where we can, finally, find peace; catch a glimpse of our divine purpose seeded in us at birth; experience a love for ourselves and others that is circular and endless; and, most of all, the only place we'll find the passage into the eternal where love's kiss awaits. So, when we're ripe, the lure becomes irresistible. And we follow. Why? Because, ultimately, some part of us knows that taming this inner wildness, finding our home in this inner landscape, will bring us to all there is to know.

And most graciously, if we persevere through the bushwhacking of our inner landscape, forging new trails toward the only true destination, we will, indeed, begin to reap sweet effects on many levels. Slowly, we'll begin to see that our experience in the outer landscape is simply a mirror reflecting the inner landscape. We've now discovered what Anais Nin knew: "We don't see the world as it is. We see it as we are."[5] And, as a result, more often, we find

---

3. Satchidananda, *Living Gita*, 193.
4. Fernao, *Buddha Quotes*, 49.
5. Nin, *Quotable Anais Nin*, 35.

Part 1: Becoming Lovers

ourselves walking out in silent communion with our God, living and breathing that peace that passes all understanding.

And, again and again, we find that paradox, the true nature of the spiritual journey, is our best friend. Whereas before we wanted to know, now we've discovered that when we're empty, silent, and open, God informs us. Where before we wanted control, now we pray to let go and let God, to surrender, so what-we-could-have-never-imagined may come through. Where before we needed proof and verification worthy of our efforts, now we sense God smiling, ready to seize our unsuspecting heart with some joy we'll never be able to fully describe or explain, but which leaves us silent, undone, unhinged, and free.

But first we have to leave the trail . . . to discover we can fly.

3

Preparing a Space

> *People travel to wonder at the height of mountains, at the huge waves of the seas, at the long course of rivers, at the vast compass of the ocean, at the circular motion of the stars . . . and they pass by themselves without wondering.*[1]
>
> SAINT AUGUSTINE

AS WE ANSWER THE call and leave the known way, we enter into our inner wilderness. Here we soon discover that it's a good idea to prepare an inner space for our explorations—a kind of crucible—within which inner transformation may occur and the necessary conditions to invite those moments of mystical unity can be held.

Ultimately, the most astonishing awareness awaits us: that *we* are, always have been, always will be the mystery, the wonder, within. What arises for you when you contemplate this amazing realization—that *you* are the wonder within? Recall the story I told in the last chapter. I didn't go outside myself to find that essence or to bring in an experience of that moment. No. Through my practice, I had trained my mind so that my soul, my eternal essence, could

---

1. Augustine, *Confessions*, 206.

Part 1: Becoming Lovers

make an appearance, however brief, from my own inner recesses. What was revealed to me, in just that half a second, came from within myself. In hindsight, it was as if it was saying, "This is who you are beyond the ramblings of your mind and storms of emotion. Be still and know!"

Just imagine. What if deep in the unexplored wilderness of your inner soul lies a secret passage into a place where silence speaks of all there is to know—a place to which we can only point—yet, once discovered, know better, trust more, than any other place we could possibly conceive of or imagine? What if, beyond all you've ever feared, beyond all your doubts, even beyond all your questions, there was a simple answer waiting, waiting for just the right moment, to cut through all you *thought* you knew to, imperceptibly, lay at your feet the one truth that informs all the others—that right there, within *you*, all along, was the treasure you've been so desperately seeking? What if you finally understood that this treasure could not be found or created—only allowed—for, in truth, it is already you?

Perhaps, then, you might just pass by yourself . . . and wonder.

So, the question becomes, "How do we find this secret passage?" Innocent enough. Understandable. Yet, the key word here that can cause intense frustration and also hinder the search greatly is *find*. This is because the passage can't be found with charted calculations. It will not appear as the result of intellectual analysis or in response to ego-driven personal will. No. Quite the contrary. This passage will only appear in moments when we're fully surrendered, empty . . . in fact, when we're, finally, no longer searching. The ultimate paradox! However, what we *can* do is prepare ourselves, prepare an inner place inside and then wait, wait to be surprised.

In the Lord's Prayer in Aramaic, the second line, traditionally translated as "Hallowed be thy name," is *Nethqadash shmakh*. "Hallowed," or *Nethqadash*, evokes images of clearing out and preparing an inner shrine to receive God's holy name, essence.[2] This clearing, releasing, letting go of all the inner clutter prepares us to hear those whispers of God and creates the conditions for moments of

---

2. Douglas-Klotz, *Prayers of the Cosmos*, 17.

Preparing a Space

sweet mystical unity. And our Mantra Prayer practice becomes the crucible for our cleansing. It's our job and joy to cleanse away what hinders our experience of our God and then to stand back and wait, wait in full delight, for that which has been there all the while waiting for us. Waiting to seize us with a love so encompassing it makes us forget to breathe. Waiting to make us lose our self so we can find our Self. Yes, it is love's kiss.

And while there are many forms of prayer and meditation that help to prepare this sacred inner space for the beloved's visit, the one we'll focus on here is Mantra Prayer. I've chosen Mantra Prayer as seekers from across faith traditions since the beginning of time have sounded their prayers to the creator and, as a result, have discovered what is expressed in the Gospel of John, 1:1, "In the beginning was the Word, and the Word was with God, and the Word was God."

Listen for the whisper.

Leave the known way.

Prepare a space ... for love's kiss awaits.

Part 2

Braving the Wilderness

4

Getting Tuned

*Divine sound is the cause of all manifestation.
The knower of the mystery of sound knows the
mystery of the whole universe.*[1]

HAZRAT INAYAT KHAN

AS LOVERS ENTER INTO the inner wilderness, their Mantra Prayer practices begin to do their work by tuning the individual spheres of consciousness, bringing them into greater harmony and resonance with the creator. Next, lovers learn important guidelines for bringing this harmony and resonance into daily life to naturally become co-creators with God. Finally, lovers begin to experience the exquisite synchronicity and wondrous freedom that arise when personal will and divine surrender become one and the same. These aspects of the inner wilderness we'll explore here in Part 2: "Braving the Wilderness."

Imagine with me an old, dusty, piano tucked away in some forgotten place. Now, in fact, we know that this neglected piano has the full potential to bring forth untold melodies. But it's been rarely played and now is desperately out of tune. Like us. We, too, are fully capable of bringing forth untold beautiful, exquisite melodies, expressing that joy that comes in the morning (see Ps 30:5). But first

1. Gass and Brehony, *Chanting*, 25.

Part 2: Braving the Wilderness

we, too, have to get tuned. So, we reach out to the master tuner: Mantra Prayer.

Let's take a closer look at how this tuning happens. Within the scope of this book, we will narrow our focus to Sanskrit, Hebrew, Aramaic, and Arabic mantra, but it's important to note that these are by no means the only languages capable of creating divine connections. But, for our purposes here, let's see how each one of these languages tunes us in our Mantra Prayer practice.

In Sanskrit mantra, used by many of the eastern faith traditions, each letter is said to be "the root vibration of material creation, maintenance, and destruction of the universe."[2] Indeed, each letter is said to represent the subtle vibrations that underlie the elements of the world. Most wondrously, as we intone Sanskrit mantra, the core sounds called seed sounds, or seed syllables, embedded in those mantra begin to bring us into harmony with the luminous spheres in the cosmos. Imagine! As we chant, we're literally aligning with and coming into greater harmony with our creator.

Similarly, in Judaism, the Hebrew letters are known as the "brick and mortar,"[3] the "protoplasm of the universe,"[4] profound, primal, spiritual forces which constitute the "raw material of creation."[5] Indeed, each of the twenty-six letters in the script is said to has a life and a meaning all its own. When put together in unique figurations to create words, the power of the words, phrases, or prayers becomes exponentially greater than just the sum of their parts. Indeed, as Rabbi Monk writes in *Wisdom in the Hebrew Alphabet*, "The combination of letters, as formulated by the spiritual masters who composed the prayers, have the power to arouse spiritual forces beyond our imagination."[6] As Christians chant in the language of Jesus, Aramaic, they discover the same mysteries as Hebrew. This is because Aramaic and Hebrew are sister languages using the same script.

---

2. Beck, *Sonic Theology*, 131.
3. Munk, *Wisdom in the Hebrew Alphabet*, 29.
4. Munk, *Wisdom in the Hebrew Alphabet*, 21.
5. Munk, *Wisdom in the Hebrew Alphabet*, 19.
6. Munk, *Wisdom in the Hebrew Alphabet*, 22.

Getting Tuned

Muslims and Sufis chant in Arabic and believe as well that revelation and grace are bestowed through the language itself, as they believe there is literally no distinction between the one chanting and the language itself. The letters of the Arabic script are said to compose the inner subtle body of each person,[7] and each letter is associated with a particular physical location in the body.[8] And, wondrously, each letter also expresses a quality or action of God recorded in the ninety-nine beautiful names Allah in the Qur'an.[9] Therefore, each of us carries within all the qualities and potentials of Allah, or God. Indeed, we could say that that each of us is, as yet, an unrealized manifestation of God himself.

For those of you interested in exploring further, I discuss in depth how the connection between us and the divine is brought about through our chanting in Sanskrit, Hebrew, Aramaic, and Arabic in my book *The Call of the Mourning Dove*. But, for now, just know that you really don't need to know to Know. In other words, if you simply do the practices, you'll be informed in ways you've yet to imagine. As St. Teresa of Availa said, "The important thing is not to think much but to love much."[10]

Now, if we're the lovers then I like to think that the sound current, embedded in the languages of the ancient mantra practices across faith traditions, is the love or the unmitigated sound of God. Ah, but this is no ordinary love that may come and go with circumstance. No, this is not an emotional love but, rather, a devotional love—so unconditional, so neutral that it rests at the still point at our very center and, most importantly, is exactly what is capable of sustaining us through life's changing conditions. Indeed, beyond what our mind may think, feel, or sense, it is truly who we are—the nature of our soul, always one with the beloved.

When we as lovers engage this love in the sound current of our mantra practice, we're actually creating the conditions to experience moments of mystical unity with our beloved God in the

---

7. Muhaiyaddeen, *Dhikr*, 21.
8. Muhaiyaddeen, *Dhikr*, 90–91.
9. Muhaiyaddeen, *Dhikr*, 21–22.
10. Teresa of Avila, *Interior Castle*, 49.

sweet silence that follows. This lover, love, beloved paradigm, first introduced in *The Call of the Mourning Dove*, I call the Sonic Trilogy of Love. In moments of mystical unity, lovers experience the indescribable, those times of deep connection with the beloved just beyond understanding. In such moments of full emersion, all distinctions between lover, love and beloved dissolve, circle in on themselves, becoming one, leaving only love. In such moments, we *become that love*, the self that was never born and never dies—the Self that eternally resides in the heart of God.

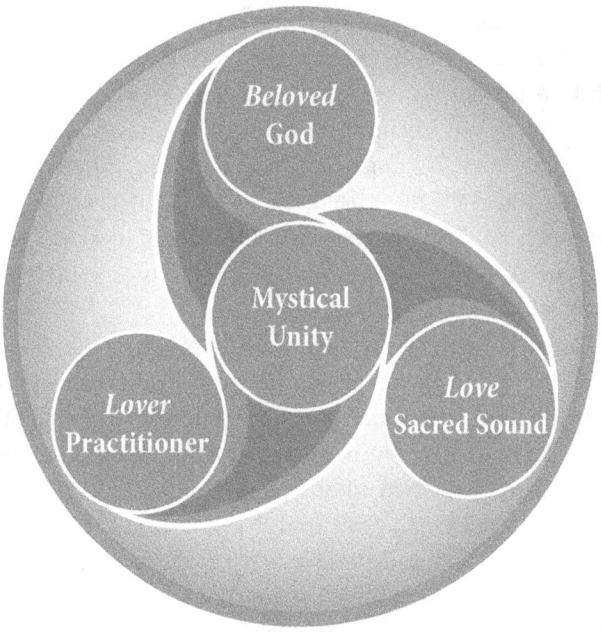

And when we start to think in terms of *being* the love instead of *finding* the love, as discussed in chapter 3, we begin to ripen into, most graciously, the awareness that *we*, as that drop in the ocean, already have, already are, the treasure itself. Whether we're chanting in Sanskrit, Hebrew, Aramaic or Arabic, our Mantra Prayer practice opens us up to this awareness by tuning and igniting our hearts, bringing us into blissful unity with our creator.

Getting Tuned

Now, let's examine more closely the two parts, mantra and prayer, and how they work together to expedite and support the tuning process. I think of mantra as our connection and prayer as our affirmation.

MANTRA: THE CONNECTION

The word *mantra* is based on the Sanskrit roots *manas*, which translates "mind," and *trai*, which translates "to set free from."[11] On a practical level, through *japa*, or repetition, mantra practice actually retrains the mind, liberating it from its old, often unhelpful habits and conditioning. It brings the unconscious parts to consciousness, transforming blocked and unhelpful energies so that those very energies may be returned back into the life force to be used in more productive ways. Einstein reminded us of this, saying that energy could not be created or destroyed.[12] It could only be transformed from one form to another.

On the esoteric level, we can better understand the mantra–mind connection as being similar to a radio. Now, there are many channels on this radio of our mind. Some just repeat the same old greatest hits from our belief system, some of which may be helpful, others not so much. Some channels just bring in the same old static or garbled chatter. But there is one channel that all mantra use that, through repetition, returns the wayward mind again and again to a point of stillness. I call this the channel of equanimity. Here the mind pauses, rests, if only for a moment, from its chronic searching. Here there's only silence and, just perhaps, the imperceptible hint of a whisper. Welcome to the entrance to the passage. Conditions are now set for you to experience, as grace may allow, moments of mystical unity with your beloved.

Realizing that we've used mantra to train the mind to bring us here to this eternal passage, we can now better contemplate the distinction between the mind and the soul. Just like the radio becomes the means for the signal but is not the signal itself, so does

---

11. Ashley-Farrand, *Healing Mantras*, 59.
12. Born, *Einstein's Theory*, 141.

the mind become the means for the soul but is not the soul itself. *We* are the soul, a drop in that ocean. *We*, in fact, are *not* our minds or our bodies.

Entering into the Sonic Trilogy of Love, we discover this again and again. For when we, as lovers, engage the love embedded in the mantra practices across faith traditions, we train the mind to rest in equanimity and, thereby, create the conditions for mystical unity with our beloved God. And, graciously, we come away knowing what, before, we could not have known.

PRAYER: THE AFFIRMATION

Just as mantra practice works on the unconscious mind, our prayerful intentions complement and support the process by working on the conscious level of the mind. By consciously using positive, prayerful thoughts, we, more often, avoid those channels on the radio of our mind that can deliver the all too common, sabotaging self-talk. If we think of prayer as simply another form of thought, or dialogue, which can support our alignment and tuning process in more helpful ways, we can rethink what it means to pray. Just remembering that *we live in God*, or that we are a drop in that ocean, can fundamentally begin to reshape our more traditional thoughts about prayer.

Let's examine this further. Those of you familiar with the great Hindu allegory, the Bhagavad Gita, know that "we live in God" is the greatest of all secrets Krishna tells Arjuna as he guides the great warrior toward victory on the battlefield of life. Yet, truth, being universal, is not contained within any one faith tradition. Saint Therese of Lisieux said it this way in her poem "The Atom of Jesus-Host": "I am the atom of Jesus . . . / . . . I have the Host as my support."[13]

So, how does this blessed awareness fundamentally reshape how we think about prayer? Well, for example, you may have wondered, with literally millions of people praying to the Lord, Jesus, Allah, Shiva, Quan Yin, or Guru Ram Das, or to many other

---

13. Therese of Lisieux, *Poetry*, 107.

representations of divine consciousness on a regular basis, how could all those prayers be held equally by any one deity? The mind struggles with this, of course, if we think of God, or the representative, as outside of ourselves. Once we remember the great secret, that we live in God, a fundamental shift happens.

Recognizing, just like Saint Therese or Arjuna, that *we too* are an atom in the body of our Jesus-Host, that *we too* live in the heart of Krishna, God personified, we start to get that it is our job to tune ourselves to the body of our blessed creator. Now, we do not pray *to* but rather *as*, as we start to get that there is nothing *out there*, outside of this heart of God in which we live, *to pray to*. No, the beloved is right here, within us, breathing us, and beating our hearts. Yet, sadly, we often scurry about here and there in constant search of that which is already within us, indeed, waiting for us, longing for us.

So, let's become lovers and brave the inner wilderness to create those conditions to receive love's kiss. Let's sit on our mats and train our wayward minds to return to equanimity, allowing for those unforeseen moments of stillness, silence, where the whisper might be heard. Let's remember, as lovers within the Sonic Trilogy of Love, it's our job to engage the love in our Mantra Prayer practice, to tune ourselves, so we may, just maybe, create the conditions to experience mystical unity with our beloved God. Let's allow our hearts to pause and just imagine that *we* are the treasure we are seeking—a fully whole and beautiful drop in the ocean of God and that the way into this grace-filled awareness is to *be* the ocean, the love, itself. And, along the way, let's imagine singing that love into our daily life, becoming that joy everlasting, in ways only our beloved God may direct.

Sit. Chant. Be.
Awe awaits.

5

Walking in Harmony

Discouraged not by difficulties without, or the anguish of ages within, the heart listens to a secret voice that whispers, "Be not dismayed; in the future lies the Promised Land."[1]

HELEN KELLER

LOVERS KNOW IT'S RARELY useful to wander around the wilderness in search of God. Instead, we go with clarity of intention into our inner wilderness for the purpose of clearing away all that stands between us and God—between us and our mind's limiting beliefs of who we think we are so we can enter into the wondrous ability to create moments of unity with our creator and experience a life of joy not predicated on outer circumstance.

This clearing, described in chapter 3, naturally occurs as we attune ourselves to the blessed creator sounding the devotional love in our Mantra Prayer practice. And, as we've seen, how wondrous to know that as we're creating the conditions for mystical unity with God, we're also clearing away all those limiting beliefs of our mind that, in our daily experience, can cause such suffering and hinder our ability to live with a sense of unity with our beloved.

---

1. Davis, *Helen Keller*, 48.

And along the way, we discover that it's actually by going straight through, not around, the felt sense of our human experience, all that suffering, that leads us to experience our divine essence. Only then do we realize that just because we believe something about ourselves doesn't mean it's true. For example, we may truly feel, "I'm not smart enough . . . good enough . . . won't be enough . . . don't have enough . . ." when contemplating our ability to go in a particular direction or to commit to some venture that's calling us. And, yes, it's absolutely true, from the vantage point of our deep humanity, that we feel this way. But, by engaging the love, the sound of God embedded in our Mantra Prayer practice, we, graciously, get to discover that, from the vantage point of our divine essence, it's not true at all. While our humanity *believes* one thing, our divinity *knows* another.

So, for example, if we sense great fear within ourselves to move forward in our life in a particular way, depending upon the circumstances, we might choose a specific Mantra Prayer practice to help cultivate courage, focus, or heal a broken heart, or to begin the process of forgiveness for ourselves or another. Notice that we're not practicing to get rid of the fear—or anything else. Instead, we're cultivating, or strengthening, a new quality. In this way, the clearing happens naturally as we engage the mind's neuroplasticity whereby, through our practice, we delete neural connections that no longer serve and strengthen new ones.

Consider a sledding analogy. Perhaps you've sledded down the same path for a very long time but one day you decide it's run its course, so to speak, so you decide to take your sled and create a new path. You simply begin creating a new path, way of thinking, way of being. There's no need to try to get rid of anything or to beat yourself up or to shame yourself. No. You simply begin creating a new path and, in doing so, your experience begins to change as now you're not just releasing, deleting, the old unhelpful neural connections and habits, you're in the process of strengthening new ones, allowing greater access to, and the expression of, your divine essence. Now, you've discovered that, far from being resignation, it's actually the radical and unmasked self-acceptance of our human journey that points us in the direction needed for clearing out what is blocking access to our full divinity.

It's in this way we become active participants in creating our experience. This is important because creating or manifesting is not a choice. It's the nature of this sphere of consciousness in which we live. In each moment, we're experiencing the effects of our previous thoughts, feelings, and actions, and, based on how we are with our present experience, we're foretelling our future. So, it makes sense that we should get about the business of becoming as conscious as possible in each moment and continue to retrain and tune the mind to support our divine essence, our soul's journey, in the most helpful way.

To live is such a blessing if we know *how*. So, before we jump into the process of creating a Mantra Prayer practice, let's consider some important guidelines discovered to be most essential to the process of staying tuned and walking in harmony with our creator as we go forward. They are elemental to Mantra Prayer, as they provide a compass for clear direction on the journey.

FIRST GUIDELINE

We create according to our conscious and unconscious beliefs. Mantra transform the energy of our beliefs creating new possibilities. Expect to be put through the tapas, or fire.

As we have said, mantra transforms unconscious, unhelpful energies into more conscious, helpful ones. In a workshop on hypnosis many years ago I witnessed one of the more striking examples illustrating the power of the unconscious beliefs on our experience. A woman in our group had just been diagnosed with a serious illness and had come seeking help. Before hypnotizing her, our instructor gave her some basic information and instruction such as, in response to questions, to lift one finger to convey *yes* and two fingers to convey *no*. Once he was satisfied that she was in a deep hypnotic state, he asked some simple questions to test her use of the finger responses. Then, at the critical moment, he asked, "Do you want to get well?" And, she raised two fingers.

To become more conscious is to get to know ourselves at deeper and deeper levels. In this way, as we move though the variety of life experiences, we can remain less a problem to ourselves. When we take up a Mantra Prayer practice, we begin to transform the old beliefs and patterns that have perpetually caused us suffering. Thankfully, these beliefs or energies, long held knotted and stagnant, can then be released and transformed to be used for a higher purpose by the healing vibration of our practice. This is why Thomas Ashley-Farrand, Namadeva Acharya, called mantra energy-based sounds. He describes the process this way in his book *Healing Mantras*: "When we pronounce mantras, we initiate a powerful vibration which corresponds to both a specific spiritual energy frequency and a state of consciousness in seed form. Over time, the mantra process begins to override all of the other smaller vibrations, which eventually become absorbed by the mantra."[2] As a result, the more unconscious places we transform, the more en*light*ened we become. We naturally become more and more transparent, relaxed, and at ease regardless of surrounding circumstances.

And this transformation happens because of *tapas*, or fire. Just as a good physical workout burns toxins from the body and intense breathwork brings up deep emotions for release, mantra practice goes to work transforming the mental energies of our unconscious belief patterns. Yet, in the midst of such transformation, as we become more and more familiar to ourselves, we can also experience great challenge. Becoming conscious requires we recognize and own our part in the creating of our experience. Because all of us are works in progress, this can be quite humbling. But, thankfully, we soon discover that it's precisely this ownership that moves us from victimhood to freedom. Ownership cultivates a kind of personal power that sets us, and everyone around us, free.

---

2. Ashley-Farrand, *Healing Mantras*, 52.

SECOND GUIDELINE

> *We may not always get what we want. We always get what we need. Every situation or outcome can teach us if we're open to receiving its gifts.*

One of the cornerstones of my teaching is *we blossom, not in spite of, but because of.* Life is challenging. It can sometimes feel unfair. God can seem to have gone AWOL. And feeling alone can be unbearable. "Why this? Why me? Why now?" we ask. And it feels like nothing but silence remains. This is not the time for philosophical discourse on the nature of the human experience. No, this is the time for tender, untethered holding of all we're feeling and enduring. In these moments, we want to be known just where we are. Analysis can come later.

And this is also the most blessed gift we can give ourselves in our daily Mantra Prayer practice. Something quite miraculous and beautiful happens when we're able to give ourselves this gift. What's occurring can begin to be held in a kind of spaciousness so it may find freedom to move through us. This loving self-acceptance of simply being with ourselves in our most challenging times is not resignation. To the contrary, acceptance allows for movement and, ultimately, release and transformation.

An important aspect I discuss with spiritual mentoring students is: *It's not about the story. It's what the story is telling us.* What does this mean? Sometimes, we get bogged down in our stories and we start to identify ourselves by them. We *become* an incest survivor, a recovering addict, a disadvantaged person from the wrong side of the tracks, a disabled veteran, and on and on. I would humbly offer here that, sadly, in doing so two things occur. First, we get quite comfortable in our self-imposed identity, allowing it to frame every understanding. Every experience begins to be seen through its lens and, as a result, life can steadily lose dimension. Secondly, being stuck in our story means we may miss the deeper spiritual lesson the experience of our story could offer us.

Recently at a community event, I was delighted to see a woman I'd not seen in a few years. Staying after, she came into my office to share with me privately. She said that she'd recently been diagnosed with leukemia. When she saw the look of shock and sadness on my face, she said, "Oh no, it's a good thing. It's in remission and, really, has been one of the best things that's ever happened to me. Because of the diagnosis, I made some important changes that I would probably not have made otherwise." She went on to tell me all about her new life and how much happier she was. I truly sensed a kind of freedom about her.

Now, I'm certain that she wouldn't have chosen the diagnosis of leukemia but, indeed, it seemed she received it as a sign of her deep need to make some difficult changes and, being deeply religious, to also cultivate an even more intimate trust in her God. Can we, too, love ourselves enough to move through our stories and ask, "What does this story, occurrence, or event have for me?"

Should we find ourselves wanting to take up a Mantra Prayer practice for healing, for example, it's important to remember that healing can occur in many different ways and on many different levels. Perhaps, as in the example above, a healing is waiting in a form we couldn't have known otherwise. And if we're able to look beyond the story or details and ask for the deeper spiritual lesson or meaning, we can rest assured that some blessed awareness will be there for us.

THIRD GUIDELINE

Be careful of just wanting to feel good.

What could possibly be wrong with just wanting to feel good? Absolutely nothing! It's always a much more desirable state than feeling bad, mad, or sad. The problem arises when deciding to feel happy, at any expense, becomes a kind of shield keeping at bay what may feel uncomfortable or threatening. The ones who keep telling themselves that their marriages are happy may not see the infidelity or divorce coming. The ones who insist their children are not capable of serious problems may not see the eating disorder until hospitalization becomes necessary. The ones who try to ignore or control excessive or compulsive behaviors may do so with devastating consequences.

Part 2: Braving the Wilderness

The degree to which we live in denial of our truth is directly related to the inevitable experience of what I call the spiritual two-by-fours. As a friend of mine who'd been in a twelve-step program for many years once said, "Before I started in AA and recovery, I would have told you I was happy and I believed it. But it took hitting rock bottom for me to really look at the truth of my life." Unfortunately, it often takes the great challenges and shocks to wake us up to what is already there.

The great challenge, as well as the true blessing, becomes practicing seeing ourselves and others as *both* human and divine—as we all are. This requires we remember that our human folly is finite and, once resolved, will return to wholeness. Our divinity, however, is always and eternally infinite. Complete unto itself. It's only in being able to hold both the human as well as the divine in ourselves and others that we may truly *see* what is occurring on a human level and then be able to *respond* from our more divine awareness in the most helpful ways.

And this practice really begins with our own self-acceptance. After all, what is true peace if not self-acceptance? And self-acceptance is the embrace of all of us, *what is*, the good parts as well as our perceived not-so-good parts. I would go so far as to say that it's the very parts we perceive to be not so good that need our love the most. As it's only in love that what is hurting or what has been marginalized can be embraced, felt, and transformed. And what is absolutely amazing is that once we begin this practice toward ourselves, we can then begin to offer it, authentically, to others. Once we stop asking ourselves to be happy or perfect or anything else other than what is simply true for us in the moment, we can more easily stop asking the same of others.

If peace is self-acceptance, then overexcitement, while intoxicating, is like a well-enjoyed addiction. While we're experiencing it, life couldn't feel better. But, inevitably, the downside follows and we're left needing the upswing again. We get trapped on the pendulum of having the desired feeling and then not having it. We may not realize there is a state where the pendulum rests and we can experience a kind of peace regardless of outer stimulation. The good news is as we give ourselves to our Mantra Prayer practice, we can gradually open to the experience of that which is eternal, that inner joy not hinged on outer circumstances, and we can finally stop settling for some outer stimulus we know is fleeting.

While doing our Mantra Prayer practice, it is most helpful to concentrate on cultivating peace and to resist gravitating toward any particular *emotional* outcome. For example, if we're struggling with an addiction, we may want to start a practice to cultivate inner courage and single-pointedness to help stay on track with our recovery. If we're having difficulties in a personal relationship, we may want to start a practice to cultivate open-heartedness as a way of seeing our self and the other with the new eyes of a compassionate heart. Notice that in both examples, we're not asking to *feel* a certain way but, rather, to cultivate a quality within that will serve us in more helpful ways.

FOURTH GUIDELINE

Don't limit your limitless potential! Always ask for "this or something better!"

This guideline opens us up to the mystery, the unexpected, and that which is often beyond our understanding. We'll be exploring this guideline in great depth in the next chapter, "Merging Will and Surrender." For now, you're invited to consider the possibility that you may not know, may not even have a clue, what may be the best path to the full manifestation of what you might imagine to be a divinely inspired life. You may have an inkling, a sense, a direction in which to point, but no clear, concrete outcome. Wonderful! I say this because one of the most important things I've been blessed to witness and experience over my many years of Mantra Prayer practice is that it is my job to follow the impulse, or direction, of my desire and then to release all attachment to the outcome or to how it might come to manifestation. In this way, the beloved has brought me outcomes I could have never imagined given my limited knowledge and understanding. By following the impulse and not already deciding on a specific outcome, we open ourselves to infinite possibilities. We're then able to attract an outcome that, in the beginning, may not have even been close to, much less on, our radar. This is why I love to say, "I'm so glad I'm not in charge of my life!" I could never have foreseen so many of the blessings I have experienced.

For example, if we are in need of a new job, it might be best to create a Mantra Prayer practice asking to attract not that perfect job we just discovered online but, rather, the most perfect job for us at this time. Now we are allowing for the possibility of attracting an even more perfect situation waiting just beyond our awareness. And the best thing is, if that job we just found online *is* the most perfect job, it will still find us! We can't lose!

When we're using a Mantra Prayer practice to attract a particular kind of outcome, let's remember to follow the impulse, the direction, and then to hold the possibility that anything we may already have in mind, the *this*, may not, in fact, come to manifestation because the *or something better* is already in store for us. This makes our life experience come alive as we, literally, give ourselves to the mystery—to bless and inform us.

And, sometimes, that blessing may not at all be what we expected or even be to our liking. In those times, we're reminded that a power greater than all of us is doing everything and that the only certainty on the spiritual journey is the realization that what we expect to happen may not. But herein lies a kind of hidden treasure if we have the eyes to see. We're now free to do what God wants *from* us instead of what we may want God to do *for* us.

FIFTH GUIDELINE

Remember that the divine source is limitless. Always intend that every request serve the greatest good for all.

We live in a competitive world. And one could observe that there's a limit to our resources. We compete to get into college, secure a new job, the next promotion, the affections of a potential mate, the eye of someone who could open doors for us, the most perfect home.

Sometimes we can feel conflicted when we desire something that's also desired by someone else. It's very freeing to remember that, on the spiritual level, there are no limitations when it comes to being provided with all we need to be content, to be productive, and to bring into manifestation our life's true purpose.

The reason for this may surprise you. Ultimately, it's because it's not about us anyway! Once we have tuned and prepared ourselves to be used as instruments for some greater purpose, it becomes a grand "Why not?" in the universe. "Why shouldn't I be provided with all I need? After all, I'm here to be an instrument of a greater good. I'm here to most humbly offer my life's purpose to the betterment of all."

Sometimes I like to think of the beloved as a well-meaning boss. Why wouldn't my boss give me all I need to do my job? And, along the way, why wouldn't I also be given all the challenges I need to cultivate the inner fortitude, awareness, and skill with which to accomplish my job as well as to meet new opportunities that will allow me to serve in an ever-expanding way? Why not, indeed!

In our Mantra Prayer practice, if we should find ourselves wanting to attract a particular outcome we know is also desired by others, let's certainly ask for what we are wanting but also set the intention that the greatest good for all be served. Let's hold a deep and abiding trust that should this particular outcome not pan out for us, it simply wasn't our assignment. It was someone else's. Our assignment is still yet to be revealed. Let's stay open and expectant so as not to miss it! This keeps us in a proactive stance and clear of the victimhood trap. Victimhood would proclaim, "Not fair! That promotion belonged to me!" Proactive faith proclaims, "Wow, there must be something even better in the works for me!"

SIXTH GUIDELINE

There is no one or nothing to compete against. Do not fight "against." Instead, fight "for."

Part 2: Braving the Wilderness

Mother Teresa, now Saint Teresa of Calcutta, once said, "I will never attend an anti-war rally. If you have a peace rally, invite me."[3] This reminds us that, energetically, we can create opposition with some other energy, within ourselves, with another person or situation, or we can go forward creating our own new energetic paths, considering the brain's neuroplasticity as we discussed earlier. One example of this is when we hear of someone fighting a disease. I would prefer to think that, instead of fighting something within myself, the part of me that is in dis-ease most likely needs my love in order to be put at ease and to be healed.

Several years ago, I was presented with a situation whereby it was suspected I could have uterine cancer. A part of my healing journey was to start sending love to my uterus around the clock. I asked the beloved to transform any dis-ease in my uterus with love, to create ease and healing. It turned out that all was well. I chose to receive it as an opportunity to practice loving myself a little better and, also, to look a little more closely at what might have been happening in my life that may have helped to attract this experience. I share this story at the end of Appendix B.

The same principle could be applied to difficulties in relationships. Instead of trying to get rid of something in ourselves or in the other, or fighting against one another, the relationship may best be served when we love ourselves and the other enough to ask for what we're needing so that a deeper love may be cultivated. When there is a mutual intention, the more difficult communications necessary for authentic healing can be better received by both parties. When no one has to be all good or all bad and when both parties assume self-responsibility for their part in creating the dynamics, both helpful and hurtful, the relationship is better able to be healed in direct response to each person's inner work and love.

So, in our Mantra Prayer practice, let's concentrate on creating new pathways of energy focusing on what we'd like to see be manifested. Let's fight *for* that which will support the most optimum expression of the divinely inspired life we are seeking.

---

3. Felton, *Peace*, 4.

SEVENTH GUIDELINE

Remember there is nothing out there. There is nothing to go get. You're not bringing anything to you. You are simply aligning yourself to receive what's already there—the hidden treasure of your divine purpose—enabling you to create a life of joy.

In addition to the realization that you already have all you need within to live a joyful, divinely inspired life, consider that you have also come into manifestation with a divine purpose. This notion is, indeed, echoed across faith traditions and spiritual literature. In the beloved Hindu scripture, the Bhagavad Gita, it is called our *svadharma*. A modern adaptation of the Bhagavad Gita, *The Legend of Bagger Vance*, calls it our authentic swing. The well-known book *The Alchemist* calls it our personal legend.

Much like the seed of a giant oak contains all that the oak may become, so do we contain in the seed of our beginnings all the potential of what we may become. This is the most extraordinary thing to realize because with this awareness we start to understand that we don't have to go get something on the outside to be more of who we may be. Rather, it is our job to cultivate what is already there within us. Yes, just like the oak seed needs water, fertilizer, and care from others, we too need our teachers, helpers, and healers. But, in the end, it's important to remember that we've already been seeded with the most perfect expression of our divine purpose. No one can give that to us, though some may be able to help us awaken to its treasure.

As we're doing our Mantra Prayer practice, let's keep in mind that all requests or intentions are, ultimately, for the purpose of nurturing this inner seed yearning to blossom and express our most sacred contract for this lifetime in service to a greater good. Let's remain content just to do our part and hold the remembrance that the full fruition of our life's purpose may not even come to full manifestation in our lifetime. As a great story from the *Tao* tells us:

Part 2: Braving the Wilderness

A traveler through the mountains came upon an elderly gentleman who was busy planting a tiny almond tree. Knowing that almond trees take many years to mature, he commented to the man, "It seems odd that a man of your advanced age would plant such a slow-growing tree!" The old man replied, "I like to live my life based on two principles: one is that I will live forever; the other is that this is my last day."[4]

---

4. Hull, "Tiny Taoist," section "2 Principles to Live By."

6

Merging Will and Surrender

> *When you have compassion and surrender to your own heart, you are surrendering to the hidden power in your heart, God. You are surrendering to love, because God is Love, the cohesive force of the universe that connects us all.*[1]
>
> SARA PADDISON

ONCE THE TUNING STARTS and we begin to walk in harmony using the guidelines to support our Mantra Prayer practice, we naturally begin to experience what I call dancing with God: moments when our personal will and divine surrender merge. Let's take a closer look.

Will	Surrender
Listen. Act in faith.	Release all outcomes to the divine.
I am enough.	I am nothing.
I follow my heart's deepest desire.	I trust the unseen hand to manifest.
I work as if it all depends on me.	I pray as if it all depends on God.
I show up.	I offer all for the greater good.

---

1. Paddison, *Hidden Power*, para. 3.

Part 2: Braving the Wilderness

ACTIVATING OUR WILL

We've been given the most precious gift and it's absolutely free. It's called *will*. And, as noted earlier, we're utilizing this gift, for better or worse, every single moment, with each thought, word, and action. It's not a choice. It *is* a choice how conscious we choose to be of the process.

Let's take a closer look at *will*. Will is very closely linked to desire. Yet, in many spiritual traditions we're told to rein in desire, primarily in relation to controlling the senses. I would offer, however, that desire is not the problem. What we choose to desire can be. For example, desiring to lead a divinely inspired life, rising every day for our Mantra Prayer practice, sitting and witnessing the whole of our experience, is the most noble of desires, though rarely the easiest path. Yet, this desire is the very one that can lead us to freedom, freedom to courageously show up to share our gifts and, ultimately, lead us to the realization that it's really not about us at all.

And, once we've started on this path, nothing else will quite satisfy. The desire to know more and more deeply this truth that makes us free (see John 8:32) expands and becomes stronger. As lovers, we fervently enter into the Sonic Trilogy of Love and dive deeper and deeper into the caverns of the heart's inner wilderness, where we know now our beloved waits and the treasure of our divine purpose may be revealed. The search propels us because as the alchemist reminds Santiago in *The Alchemist*, "Wherever your heart is, there you will find your treasure. And, you've got to find the treasure so that everything you have learned along the way can make sense."[2] And so, we commit to our Mantra Prayer practice to embrace the full truth of our experience and to tune the mind just long enough to perhaps hear, from the deep recesses of our heart, that whisper pointing us toward our sweet treasure. It's the only way our deepest longing can be satisfied.

And once we begin to sense that silent voice, nudging us in a particular way or direction, *and* we allow ourselves to hear it, something happens. A kind of vortex of energy is activated and, as events unfold, we find ourselves being both actor and witness,

2. Coelo, *Alchemist*, 116.

Merging Will and Surrender

moving along on our human journey yet observing ourselves being carried by something much larger than we can perceive.

This is why, once our will has been activated in a particular direction, it's crucial to *release* the manifestations of our inner treasure into the hands of the beloved. It's why it's important to remember that it's truly faith that moves mountains, not reason. As we read in *The Traveler's Gift*, "Reason can only go so far—faith has no limits."[3] Let's believe in what is possible and open to the mystery just waiting to inform us.

Now we're realizing that the best use of our will is that it be put in service to the nudges of our deepest love, the whisperings of our beloved pointing us toward our inner treasure, as now we know that such whisperings are calling us to some greater service of which we, most often, only know a part. But no matter. It's just our job to step up and do our part in full faith and trust and, smiling, invite our finite mind to contemplate, "All things are possible to him who believes" (Mark 9:23).

ALLOWING SWEET SURRENDER

"Surrender" is a loaded word in our culture. But, as usual on the spiritual path where paradox is the rule, it's surrender that actually predisposes us to receiving that which is infinitely sweeter than anything we could have imagined. Surrender is where the mystery unfolds. With surrender our task is not to *do* anything but rather to *be*, allowing God to work through us.

In the broadest sense, sweet surrender with God can happen at any time in our daily life, such as in an unexpected encounter on the bus home, in the grocery store, waiting in line to check out. Its rhythm teaches us a kind of trust that brings a growing realization that all is truly unfolding as it should—that we're placed each moment exactly where we need to be to give what we need to give and to receive what we need to receive. It's an awesome thing to realize that, in the eyes of God, all occurrences are equally important to the creation of the divine plan. As Mother Teresa once said, "Do

---

3. Andrews, *Traveler's Gift*, 167.

Part 2: Braving the Wilderness

small things with great love," because, "to God, nothing is small; the moment we have given it to God, it becomes infinite."[4]

Yet, as we know, life can be extremely challenging. What of those times? We might ask, "What do you mean all things work for good for them that love God?" (see Rom 8:28). These are the times when our faith can be deeply challenged. Yet, as we are able to surrender the circumstances of our life into God's hands, a kind of peace begins to settle, that peace that passes all understanding (see Phil 4:7).

One of my favorite examples of this is from the true story of a couple named Doolittle whose presence inspired the writing of the well-loved hymn "His Eye is on the Sparrow." Here is the story as told by Civilla D. Martin:

> Early in the spring of 1905 my husband and I were in Elmira, New York. We developed a deep friendship for a couple by the name of Mr. and Mrs. Doolittle—true saints of God. Mrs. Doolittle had been bedridden for nearly 20 years. Her husband was an incurable cripple who had to propel himself to and from his business a wheelchair. . . . Despite their afflictions, they lived happy lives bringing inspiration and comfort to all those who knew them. One day while we were visiting with the Doolittles, my husband commented on their bright hopefulness and asked them for the secret of it. Mrs. Doolittle replied simply, "His eye is on the sparrow, and I know He watches me." [See Matt 6:26.][5]

In full surrender, we don't need conditions to be a certain way in order to love God. Our love becomes truly unconditional. We love because it's simply the only option. And it sets us free.

---

4. Saint Mark Catholic Church, "Other Art," section "Millennium Saints: Blessed Mother Teresa of Calcutta."

5. Terry, "Story Behind the Song," paras. 7–8.

INTEGRATING WILL AND SURRENDER

There is a beautiful saying from Tao philosophy: "To know when you can get no further by your own action, that is the right beginning."[6] It all begins with a fundamental question we can ask ourselves: What do I want? Do I want to belong to the world, spending my days in service to my own desires and needs or do I want to belong to God, spending my days in service to a greater good? Swamis in the yoga tradition often describe the latter as being *in* the world *but not of* the world. Sometimes we think we'd like to be instruments but may feel too rusty or out of tune to presume to carry such grace. So, simple desire isn't enough. What's required is getting tuned through our Mantra Prayer practice so, over time, our sweet treasure may shine through.

And, in such moments of harmony, when our will and surrender are fully aligned, we become what I like to call a *living* Mantra Prayer. We *know* we're a drop where the full essence of the cosmic ocean merges. We *know* the great secret to living a divinely inspired life: we live in the heart of God. We *know* we have been seeded with a divine purpose and with all we need to bring it forth.

In such moments of knowing, we experience exactly what Jesus asked of us in Matthew 5:48, "Be ye perfect even as your Father in heaven is perfect." Perfect, you say. And why not? Perfection as an instrument has nothing to do with perfection as our ego might imagine it. In fact, it's exactly in such moments of pure attunement that we instantly get it's not about us at all! As Krishna reminds Arjuna in the Bhagavad Gita, we too are just here to fulfill a purpose, to play a part, to get something done, and to, along the way, fully experience that we too are, graciously, a spark of the light of all lights forever beyond darkness (see Sloka 13:17).[7]

As a living Mantra Prayer, we activate our will to move in the direction of our deepest love, impulse, and delight and surrender any outcome to the mystery, knowing that what may be revealed or manifested will very likely bring a sweet surprise we could have

---

6. Zhuangzi, https://www.azquotes.com/quotes/topics/taoism.html.
7. Satchidananda, *Living Gita*, 193.

never imagined. Life then becomes alive, fun, wondrous, and holy beyond measure.

Brave the wilderness.

Tune.

Dare to be a lover . . . sounding the love to create the conditions for the beloved's kiss.

Claim your birthright . . .

as an atom in the body of all creation.

Step out like a shepherd . . .

activating your will propelled by your beloved's inner whisper.

Surrender all to the mystery.

And create a life of beauty beyond your imagination.

Part 3

Singing the Holy

7

Preparing Your Spiritual Practice Crucible

Submit to daily practice. Your loyalty to that is a ring on the door. Keep knocking, and the joy inside will eventually open a window and look out to see who's there.[1]

BAWA MUHAIYADDEEN

ENTERING INTO THE SONIC Trilogy of Love, becoming lovers in our inner wilderness, is not for the fainthearted. Sitting in the crucible of our compassionate heart as all that's in the way of our full experience of God, our true Self, is burned away can be extremely challenging. So here in Part 3, "Singing the Holy," you'll be shown how to create a strong crucible in preparation for your practice, be led through a step-by-step process to create your Mantra Prayer practice, and be shown how to navigate all the obstacles that will certainly appear.

It's in our spiritual practice where we, indeed, *practice* cultivating that presence to be used as instruments of divine grace. Experiencing moments of sweet bliss, peace, equanimity, even mystical unity, reveals that we're a part of something much larger, that-which-is-beyond-understanding, the eternal presence of our

---

1. Barks and Green, *Illuminated Prayer*, 38.

beloved God. And as we move through our human emotions, transforming the darkness of our inner wilderness, we practice bringing this eternal presence to ourselves—and, ultimately, as a result, find we can authentically offer it to others.

As we become more present in our daily life, we naturally recognize those moments of reaction, moments of being unceremoniously pulled off our center of presence and equanimity. And before we know it, we're right in the playpen having a grand old time—and, soon, feeling shaken and awful. Wonderful! Yes! Because now we have something to take to our practice and have been given an opportunity to clear and transform one more place in the unconscious, the darkness, making us such a problem to ourselves.

Still, there can also be long periods of time where it seems we're consistent and committed but don't sense anything really happening . . . until something unforeseen occurs and we find ourselves thinking, "Wow! If that had happened six months ago, I'd have responded very differently." So, regardless of whether we find challenge or confirmation in our daily life, our spiritual practice becomes the place where we become like alchemists, learning to transform the lead of the journey into gold. So, let's take a look at the key elements in creating your spiritual practice crucible.

PREPARING YOUR CRUCIBLE

It's fitting that the first step in creating your Mantra Prayer practice is to prepare a crucible to contain the *tapas*, or heat, necessary for the alchemy to come. This is first symbolized by the outer elements, or structure, of your practice. Over time, the body itself becomes the primary crucible as the *tapas* of mantra practice begins to do its work. Let's look at the components of your spiritual practice crucible.

Your Special Place

I've noticed over the years as I've helped individuals to commit to spiritual practice that this initial step can often bring up the first levels of resistance and challenge, particularly for those new to

Preparing Your Spiritual Practice Crucible

spiritual practice. What'll my family think if I create an altar or sacred space? What might visitors think?

Creating a special space for practice ultimately becomes a kind of statement of what's important to us. At a fundamental level, it's an affirmation of what we want our lives to be about. And, it's important to know that, as we make conscious shifts, others around us are affected as well. So, I always suggest, if this is a new step, talk openly with those with whom you live. Share just what you're doing and why. Ask for their support. People are much more willing to accommodate a change if they're included in the reason and in the process. Conversely, it's often secrecy that breeds suspicion and feeds resistance.

I'd recommend choosing a relatively small area, something private that feels intimate. I've known those who've used a part of a room or have converted large closets, attics, or basement spaces for their practice. Once you've chosen a place, you can decide if you'd like to use a meditation cushion or bench or a chair. Finally, you can consider whether you'd like a small table or, perhaps, would prefer to just lay out your special items on a mat before you.

Special items you might choose often include pictures or statues representing a divine incarnation with whom you resonate, pictures of important spiritual teachers. Some form of prayer beads is also essential. These might include a mala used in many Eastern faith traditions, Christian rosary, Eastern Orthodox prayer rope, or Sufi-Muslim tasbih. Include any variety of additional objects that hold special meaning for you such as items from nature, pictures of family, special items you've collected, or spiritual gifts you've received along the way. Finally, additional items you may also want to include are: shawl or blanket, digital music source, timer, journal, book light for dark mornings, special readings, tissues, and an eye pillow. This is *your* space. Create it so it may support your spiritual journey!

Part 3: Singing the Holy

The Time to Start

The great majority of spiritual traditions recommend we practice during what are called the ambrosia hours, from 4:00 a.m. to about 6:00 a.m. Mother Teresa and the Sisters of Charity, many Buddhist orders, Hindus, and Sikhs all begin at 4:00 a.m. Mohandas Gandhi and George Washington Carver both rose at 4:00 a.m. George Washington Carver reflected, "All my life I have risen regularly at four o'clock and have gone into the woods and talked with God. There he gives me my orders for the day.... After my morning's talk with God I go into my laboratory and begin to carry out his wishes for the day."[2] When asked how he got the peanuts, sweet potatoes, and flowers to give us their secrets, he answered, "Anything will give up its secrets if you love it enough . . . people give up their secrets also—if you love them enough."[3] We, too, give up our secrets when we love ourselves enough.

But truth is, rising at 4:00 a.m. every day, while certainly not impossible, is very challenging outside the confines of monastic life. Though I sincerely committed to doing so for many years, I finally had to admit that, because of teaching at night, I simply needed more sleep. So, now I rise and begin as it feels right for me. I do, however, make a special effort during the long winter months to rise particularly early as I just don't think there's anything sweeter than doing my practice in complete darkness.

While I always recommend a morning practice, it's most important to invite the practice to flow easily with the realities of your daily life. Many years ago, one of my students moved up to the central part of the state and very much wanted to do the Bhagavad Gita Certificate Program via correspondence. I confess I was skeptical as one of the program requirements was to commit to a spiritual practice, and this particular student had four children under the age of ten! As we talked, she shared that with a fairly new baby, mornings were out, and by evening she was just too tired. But she was absolutely committed to going forward. So, I encouraged her to talk with her husband to see if some other time could be worked out. Together,

---

2. Clark, *Man Who Talks*, 21–22.
3. Clark, *Man Who Talks*, 22–23.

they decided that the first hour upon his return home from work would be best as he could then spend time with the children. For all of them, though sometimes challenging, it worked out and she completed the program, something for which she was very proud.

Sometimes when I'm feeling resistant to doing my practice, I'll think of her and feel instantly inspired! It reminds me again of the question, "What do we *really* want?"

Number of Days for a Practice

Many faith traditions teach that it takes at least forty days to begin to bring about a change in the psyche and in life experience. So, I always recommend that a new practice be continued for at least forty, uninterrupted, days. The number forty, of course, has biblical roots. In the Old Testament, Moses spends forty days and forty nights on Mount Sinai (see Exod 34:28), and Jesus was tested in the wilderness for forty days and nights (see Matt 4:1–11). One could say that the mount, or the wilderness, metaphorically represents the inner sanctuary—the crucible within which we do our work.

Rarely, once I've committed to a forty-day duration, do I stop a particular mantra practice. Even if I'm feeling resistance to continuing or, for some reason, don't feel the practice is serving me as I might have hoped, I almost always try to continue for the forty days. The reason is simple. The mind can be quite seductive and persuasive when faced with giving up some long-held patterns. It'll fight for its very survival. This is why I like to tell my mind, "Thank you for sharing. Now, kindly go sit!" Without fail, particularly when I'm sensing clear resistance, if I can discipline myself to persevere, I've found some important awareness waiting for me just on the other side. Conversely, more often, I've started a forty-day practice only to discover that the mantra is not done with me after such a short time. It's the sweetest feeling to be held fast by a mantra practice. Some practices have held me for many months before loosening their grip. Not to worry. You'll know when it's time to leave a practice, for, in truth, it'll be done with you, at least for the time being.

PART 3: SINGING THE HOLY

Number of Repetitions for a Practice

In addition to the minimum forty-day recommendation for a practice, different faith traditions lean toward using a specific number of mantra repetitions in spiritual practice. To keep track of the number of repetitions, prayer beads are often used as noted above. The mala used by many Eastern faiths has a hundred and eight beads correlating with the major nadis, or nerves, of the subtle body. The mala used by Muslims and Sufis, the misbaha or tasbih, has ninety-nine beads for the ninety-nine beautiful names of Allah in the Qur'an. The Christian rosary has fifty-four beads used to recite traditional prayers to the Blessed Mother. Depending upon the faith tradition and the sacred phrases being repeated, a varying number of repetitions may be recommended for cultivating particular intentions.

Now that you've prepared your spiritual practice crucible, it's time to create your Mantra Prayer practice.

8

Creating a Mantra Prayer Practice

*You create a path of your own by looking
within yourself and listening to your soul,
cultivating your own ways of experiencing the
sacred and then practicing it. Practicing until
you make it a song that sings you.*[1]

SUE MONK KIDD

"MAKE IT A SONG that sings you." This is the ultimate goal of our spiritual practice. We sing in our spiritual practice to hear in the silence that follows the sweet whisper of our beloved God. As this experience grows within us, we find ourselves, more often, being sung in our daily life. We push and strive less because we recognize now *Lo Echsar*, as we discussed in chapter 1. We lack not. We're already full. We're more present to ourselves and others so we can be available to be used as instruments of divine grace at any moment in daily life.

So now that you've created the crucible for your Mantra Prayer practice, you're ready to design the practice itself. Below is a model I've used and have offered many as a starting place for designing. Based on your experience with spiritual practice and whether or not you're accustomed to using practices from one or from multiple

---

1. Kidd, *Dance*, 224.

faith traditions, you may want to adapt the model to better accommodate your unique practice needs.

As most of us, at different times in our life experience, may want to cultivate healing, forgiveness, courage, focus, or abundance, I've chosen these general categories and have selected Mantra Prayer practices from Judaism, Christianity, Sufism, Hinduism, Buddhism, and Sikhism which help to cultivate these qualities. You'll find them, along with sample breath practices, in Appendix A. Now let's begin creating your practice!

STEP 1: STATE WHAT HAS BROUGHT YOU TO A SPIRITUAL PRACTICE AT THIS TIME.

This is a general assessment of what has brought you to create a Mantra Prayer practice. It's totally okay not to know or to just come with a general curiosity or with a feeling of just wanting to begin something positive for yourself. More often than not, however, we do come to our practice with the desire to heal or transform in some way. This sense of what is bringing us to our practice is usually an acknowledgment of *what is* in our human journey. It's best found by following your *feelings*. Remember, your full acknowledgment is exactly what's first required to transform any existing condition. So, this is the crucial beginning. Still, remember that acceptance is not resignation. In addition, it may also be an opportunity to discern just what is yours and what is not, what you have control over and what you do not, particularly in relation to others.

Some initial recordings of what has brought you to a practice at this time using the categories we've identified might be:

> Healing: "I'd like to recover from . . ."
> Forgiveness: "I'd like to forgive myself for . . . or [name] for . . ."
> Courage: "I'd like to feel stronger . . . be more self-assured . . ."
> Focus: "I'd like to be more focused . . . clear . . . unwavering . . ."
> Abundance: "I'd like to live in full faith and trust that all I need to support my path will naturally be provided . . ."

CREATING A MANTRA PRAYER PRACTICE

STEP 2: WRITE YOUR PRAYERFUL INTENTION.

Your intention is your prayer to support your Mantra Prayer practice. Remember that this prayer is a conscious thought affirming that your heart's deepest desire and thoughts are power. The whole of your experience is birthed through your inner self-talk. Recalling our discussion on working with will and surrender, this is where you use your will to focus your mind with clear intention. General guidelines for helping you to create conscious prayerful intentions are:

- Start with *Thank you!* Gratitude effortlessly opens the crucible within for exactly what's waiting to happen. Start with heartfelt gratitude and everything else will take care of itself.
- State your intention in the present tense. You're affirming for yourself what you desire, right here and now, not begging for an outside source to comply at some point in the future.
- Affirm your desire for everyday concrete items or things, like a particular car. For the more important things, such as a new job, relationship, or opportunity, always affirm the impulse but leave the outcome inductive, or open, for the beloved to bring forth what may not even be on your radar.
- Commit to supporting your intentions with energy that's steady and joy-filled with expectation.

And now for specific examples of prayerful intentions using our designated categories:

- Healing intention: Instead of "I'd like to cure . . ." say, "Thank you for healing energy with every breath I take." Focus on what you'd like to create not get rid of.
- Forgiveness intention: Instead of "I forgive [name] for . . ." say, "I release all feelings of hurt, anger or resentment. For my part in creating any ill will, I am sorry. Please forgive me. May we both be happy. May we both be free. Thank you." This example is inspired by the beautiful Ho'oponopono Hawaiian practice for forgiveness.

- Courage intention: Instead of "I'd like to get strong enough to leave my job, go back to school, start that business . . ." say, "Thank you for strength and courage to speak and act my truth as necessary. I attract and receive the most perfect job/school/business opportunity to use my gifts in service to the greater good. I welcome all joys and challenges as I learn and grow." You are affirming that you have the full potential to actualize that which you are seeking.

- Focus intention: Instead of "I'd like the job at ABC Company . . ." say, "Thank you for opening my awareness to receive the best job for me." Think inductively, not deductively. This or something better! Remember the beloved may have something in store for you that may not even be on your radar!

- Abundance intention: Instead of "I'd like to receive [particular dollar amount] . . ." say, "Thank you for supplying me with all the monetary income I presently need. I remain open and receptive as to how I may participate in attracting this abundance." This example relates to money, but remember this same intention could be altered slightly to address other areas of abundance you may be wanting. Affirm your birthright to be fully supported in all ways by your creator. Assume and expect that you'll be supplied with all you need to live joyfully and abundantly as you follow your divine path.

STEP 3: SELECT A BREATH MEDITATION AND MANTRA PRAYER PRACTICE.

At this point, you'll want to check out Appendix A and select a breath meditation and Mantra Prayer practice that will help you to cultivate your prayerful attention. You'll notice I've given each of the qualities a number and included the appropriate number(s) for each mantra practice so you can make an educated choice. You can also hear them under "Audio Books" on my website: https://stephanierutt.com. Sometimes in hearing them we can feel the one that's choosing us. Then, I'd recommend selecting a breath practice from the same faith tradition.

Before sitting in your practice, it's good to move your body in some way with gentle stretches, yoga postures, or perhaps a walking meditation with which you are familiar. Then follow with breathwork to cleanse and stabilize the emotional body. Breathwork is a vital preparation before working with a mantra. Now you are ready to begin your mantra repetition to work with your mental body to retrain the mind and transform unhelpful energies into more helpful ones. With some form of physical movement, breath, and mantra, you're engaging the physical, emotional, and mental bodies aligning them to serve as a portal into the spiritual body where your beloved waits.

STEP 4: SIT IN SILENCE.

Following the chanting of your Mantra Prayer comes *the* most important part of your practice: sitting in silence. You may do this with simple sitting or also by engaging traditional meditation practice or centering prayer practice. Sitting in silence is crucial because you have now created the conditions to *hear in the silence that follows* from a deeper place in your being. Up until this point, you've been using your will, doing your part to prepare, to tune yourself. Now, you're ready to fully surrender and receive the fruits of your practice. As Mother Teresa once said, "God speaks in the silence of the heart and we listen."[2] As a lover, you've entered into the Sonic Trilogy of Love to intone the love, the sacred sound current within the sacred practices, to join in holy communion with your beloved, and, as a result, to just perhaps experience a moment of mystical unity with your creator.

2. Spink, *Mother Teresa*, 74.

PART 3: SINGING THE HOLY

STEP 5: RESTATE YOUR INTENTION AND JOURNAL.

Finally, I always recommend ending your Mantra Prayer practice with restating your intention. It brings you full circle and to completion. Following, you may enjoy journaling in a spiritual practice journal to record the unfolding of your experience. I and many others with whom I've practiced have found journaling to be an extremely valuable exercise to processing the experience. Over time, you can look back and see how far you've come.

YOUR FINAL MANTRA PRAYER SPIRITUAL PRACTICE SEQUENCE

- Acknowledge what has brought you to a spiritual practice at this time.
- State your prayerful intention.
- Move the body: simple stretching, Yoga, Kriya, walking meditation.
- Breathe: breath meditation, 5+ minutes.
- Sing/chant: Mantra Prayer practice, 10+ minutes.
- Sit in silence: 10+ minutes.
- Restate your intention.
- Journal as desired.

9

Navigating through Obstacles

A clay pot sitting in the sun will always be a clay pot. It has to go through the white heat of the furnace to become porcelain.[1]

MILDRED WITTE STOUVEN

WE'RE THE CLAY POT. Our spiritual practice is the kiln. As we go through the white heat of the furnace, we practice surrendering all that masks our true form. It's important to remember that being our most divine self is not the hard part. The hard part is allowing all that isn't necessary to be burned away in the kiln of our compassionate heart.

And, as we've said, this is very often quite challenging. On the human level, we may have deep wounds to cleanse for true healing. On the spiritual level, we may fear our freedom most. After all, we may wonder, "What'll it truly mean for me to get tuned by the divine hand? How will I, my life, change?"

Still, if you're reading this book, you can bet that there's some insatiable longing of your heart that will not allow you to fritter your days away any longer. Yet, with all our longing, the kiln is not an easy place to reside. We know this. So, the minute we decide to commit to a Mantra Prayer spiritual practice, all the inner

---

1. Struven, "QuotesLyfe," line 1.

obstacles show up to the party! No, they wouldn't miss this one for the world! Yet, how *lucky for us* as now we have the opportunity to acknowledge, embrace, and, ultimately, transform them—all those old wounds, patterns, feelings, beliefs, and behaviors that keep us from the full awareness and experience of the inner porcelain of our divinity.

And we know that what we resist simply persists. So, we practice creating a space of humble, spacious surrender for holding whatever may be arising in the moment. And, little by little, we find that as we face the dragons of our deepest fears, their power diminishes in direct response to our resolve. This is when we discover that all those inner caves we've so feared to enter truly do hold the very treasures we're seeking. For there, as we discover the true essence, the illusionary fears of our humanity, we naturally open to the true essence of our inner divinity.

Let's look at the more common obstacles identified most comprehensively by practitioners of *Vipassana*, mindfulness, meditation rooted in the Buddhist faith tradition. There are five, and, in my experience, they most often represent the deeper levels of resistance expressed through our individual experiences. The first and second are often considered as pairs, as are the third and fourth, and the fifth follows, though, in true experience, the obstacles often blend in an infinite variety of ways.

DESIRE AND AVERSION

It's the nature of the mind to run *to* what we desire or pleases us and to run *from* what is undesirable or painful. Let's look at desire first. This one we touched on earlier. It can be tricky because it is absolutely our birthright to be happy! "So, what could be so wrong with that?" you ask. The problem is not with feeling good. The trouble comes when we predicate our happiness on circumstances outside of ourselves. If we're having a good day, we're happy. If we're having a bad day, we're angry or sad. However, if we understand that all forms and seasons of our emotional life serve to help us know ourselves a little better, we can begin to experience the difference between happiness hinged on outside circumstances and the joy resting undisturbed, through all our emotional seasons, at our very center. This inner joy is better described as a still point, quiet peace, mentioned earlier, that the Bible says passes all our understanding (see Phil 4:7).

Desire can take on an infinite number of expressions. Invariably, it kicks in to fulfill some need the ego has designated as important and then we strive to have that particular need met. Yet, I've noticed that the more I get to know the inner joy, the less striving I do. I define myself less by what I may possess or by what I may accomplish and more by my inner state of being. Some place of deep trust begins to awaken when I remember that I'm truly enough in any situation regardless of what I may or may not possess or may or may not know. When I'm tuned in to the joy of my inner sanctuary and stop relying solely on my ability to figure things out or to present myself in a certain way, I begin to dance with God. And this dance is infinitely sweeter than any personal desire or achievement I may fulfill.

It's not that we don't enjoy nice things, seek to advance ourselves in our work, engage actively in spiritual practice, or serve our community. What is different is that we are, more often, guided by an inner compass and not by the arbitrary requirements set by our environment. We're not striving for external recognition. Rather, we're praying to get tuned to become instruments of the divine song.

Now, let's look at desire's twin, aversion. Yes, twin, because they're opposite sides of the same coin. They go together. For example, when we desire something and don't get it, what happens? Also, if we desire a new home or the next degree, principally to gain outer recognition, then we're likely to set up what I call the *I'll be happy when* syndrome. I'll be happy when I have that new house, graduate, get that great job or promotion, find the right person, have children, lose weight, and so on. If we achieve, we're happy. If we fall short, we feel less successful or incomplete. Again, it's not that we shouldn't fully enjoy all of these things. But there is a difference between enjoying things and needing them to help us feel complete. Remember, the truth is we're already complete—right where we are!

PART 3: SINGING THE HOLY

But aversion, all by itself, is perhaps the most formidable of obstacles. Just as we can see no problem with wanting to be happy, we certainly can see no good reason for venturing into our inner wilderness, particularly when we're not certain what we may find there. This is a good time to remember that the whole purpose of spiritual practice is to bring the unconscious to consciousness, to transform our dense, dark, unknown places to leave us a little lighter. This is what it means to become en*light*ened.

The more we resist our aversions, the more often we find the mind as our jailer, holding us hostage to all we fear. In the Christian allegory *Hinds' Feet on High Places* by Hannah Hurnard, the protagonist, Much Afraid, wants nothing more than to follow the Good Shepherd to the high places. Along the way, when her fears surface in response to the appearance of her cousin Craven Fear, who wants to capture her and take her back home, the Good Shepherd warns sternly:

> "Much Afraid, don't ever allow yourself to begin trying to picture what it will be like. Believe me, when you get to the places which you dread you will find that they are as different as possible from what you have imagined. I must warn you that I see your enemies lurking among the trees ahead and if you ever let Craven Fear begin painting a picture on the screen of your mind, you will walk in fear and trembling and agony where no fear is."[2]

"Where no fear is." This is why the forces of darkness, ignorance, and fear are often referred to as illusion. Yes, it's true that we believe, feel, and experience them and, yet, they are all a fabrication of our mind, not in any way related to our true divine self at all. And this is exactly why when we have the courage to face what we might rather avert, the illusion we've so closely held simply dissipates right before our eyes.

And so we sit and observe the daily parade of thoughts, some happy, some sad, some good, some bad. And, along the way, we discover, again and again, that they are just that—thoughts parading across the screen of our mind.

---

2. Hurnard, *Hinds' Feet*, 145.

Navigating through Obstacles

SLEEPINESS AND RESTLESSNESS

We live in a very fast paced society, and many of us simply don't get enough sleep. So, sometimes, when we stop long enough to listen, we hear our bodies crying for more rest. However, if sleepiness becomes a common response during our meditation practice, then it's likely that some form of zoning out is occurring. All of us have adapted ways to protect ourselves from painful feelings. It's how many of us survived difficult childhoods. Yet, what might have served us well then, keeps us from the full experience of our self now.

It has been both my experience and observation that when we have a wound we build our entire lives around hiding and protecting that wound. Those of us who have engaged in this behavior know well how very much energy it takes to construct and continuously present a persona that we hope the world will buy as us. And, if we do so long enough, we can even end up believing our own fabrication. As we come into our practice, returning to the present moment again and again, our carefully constructed persona begins to self-destruct. Thank God! But this can feel very frightening, often more so than need be, because the mind holds a whole set of beliefs about how and what it's all going to be like when we have the courage to come into the truth. So, the challenge is to stay awake (no pun intended!) to whatever is arising in the present moment and not allow the mind to just arbitrarily paint a picture on the screen of our mind—where no fear is.

The twin of sleepiness is restlessness. As with sleepiness, restlessness often shows up in a physical manifestation. But I have discovered that any physical restlessness I'm experiencing is directly related to my mental and emotional state. The mind will pull out all the stops as we try to harness its wayward ways. "Ok, you've decided that you're going to sit for ten minutes, but I'm going to continue doing my thing. So, let's plan our day, or rehash that difficult conversation you had yesterday, or, even better, let's construct some great fantasy for the future!" Yes, the mind will want to be anywhere but in the present moment! This is because the mind is part of God's changing, manifested expression residing in the context of time and space. The mind knows best the past and the future. It's much less familiar with how to come into the present moment and become the portal to our inner divinity.

And, as long as the seductive mind is doing its thing, the great reward for us is that we are saved, once again, from the deeper, less safe waters of our inner landscape. Whew! Escaped again! And so we stay enslaved, thinking we are free.

DOUBT

This one's so big it gets to have its own category. Doubt is the mind's trump card. If all else fails, this one will do it! First let's look at what doubt is not. Doubt is not healthy discernment. Healthy discernment pays attention to inner feelings and responses, seeks to observe with a sense of focused neutrality, questions thoughtfully, and disagrees respectively. Discernment clearly sees what is and what is not and enables a response that is both authentic and compassionate.

Doubt, as an obstacle to spiritual practice, tends to originate from deeply held beliefs formed as a result of our familial and environmental conditioning. Doubt is very wary of suspending such beliefs or opening to new experiences where the existing thought patterns might be challenged. Doubt often leans toward intellectualizing, overanalyzing, and proving points based upon past observations and experiences. It looks for proof and wants to see concrete cause-and-effect relationships. Doubt wants to know the territory before stepping in and wants to be assured of outcomes or, at the very least, be offered reasonable explanations when expected results do not materialize. Doubt makes it easy to just walk away.

The trouble is, the evolution of consciousness does not unfold to the mind's specifications.Whether you believe in reincarnation and the evolution of the soul through the law of karma or simply believe in that mystery that passes all our understanding, at some point it dawns that a lot is going to happen to us and around us for which there may never be any reasonable or rational explanation. However, while we may not be able to predict what occurs in our life experience, we can always determine what we will do with what occurs. This simple truth can steer us away from victim consciousness and from the accompanying pervasive doubt it creates and toward a more self-responsible consciousness that remembers we can choose to be alchemists, turning the most difficult experience into a treasure of learning. Alchemists tend to grow wise. Those who doubt tend to grow old.

And as doubt holds us hostage and paints the old familiar patterns across the screen of our mind, inevitably our commitment weakens.

And our inner treasures waits.

MIND PICTURES

Below are just a few of the more common strategies we tend to paint across the screen of our mind related to the five obstacles. I call them mind pictures.

Desire:

> "How spiritual I'm going to be when I adopt a daily practice!"
> *Well, maybe. But along the way, you're more likely to get in touch with your deep humanity.*
> "Finally, I have some tools to create my life just as I want!"
> *True . . . but God may have other plans. Can you surrender to these?*
> "Ooooo, I just love the buzz I get with this mantra. I must really be getting it now!"
> *Buzz is sweet but sweeter still is how we treat our neighbor . . . our enemy.*
> "I'm going to have a really great day, feel good, now that I've meditated. Everything's just going to be much better now!"
> *Yes, we're often positively affected by our meditation practice. And, also, like cleaning out a deep wound,*

sometimes things can feel worse on the way to feeling better. But if this is happening, the good news is that healing is on the way!

Aversion:

"If I feel anger or sadness that means I'm not spiritual."

No feeling is ever bad or wrong. In fact, allowing and honoring our deepest, most difficult feelings is the first step to true self-acceptance and self-love. Once our deep humanity is embraced, then the denser energies may be transformed and rechanneled in more productive ways.

"I'm afraid to feel what I feel. What if I drown in sadness or lose control?"

This is perhaps "the" biggest illusion. What can hold us captive for an entire lifetime can begin to be struck down the instant we have the courage to turn and face it.

"No one has ever really suffered like I have. No one will truly understand."

Having been a healing practitioner for many years, I'm convinced that we each have our share of challenge and sadness. While our stories and experiences differ, we can each relate to the same deep feelings.

"Life is unfair. That's just how it is. There's nothing you can do about it."

It's your choice. You can be a victim or you can be like the lotus flower and blossom, not in spite of, but because of.

Sleepiness:

"Forget this! Let's go shopping, have a few, raid the refrigerator, surf the net, get that report done, clean the house. I've got a million things I'd rather be doing or certainly should be doing!"

We each have ways we've adapted to help us zone out from pain and difficulty. Acknowledging our particular way is the first step to transforming it.

"I don't know about this 'becoming spiritual' stuff. What'll it really mean for my life?"

Any shift we make within ourselves causes a shift in our relationships. Yet, the ones who truly love us will want for us what we want for our self.

Restlessness:

"I've got to visualize a better way! Hey, all of life is just a response to our thoughts, right?"

True. But remember, there is the creator who knows what we're needing and wanting even before we speak.

"You know, I've really got a great life already. I really don't need to go fishing for troubles!"

Sometimes facing our deep fears takes time. And part of loving our self is honoring the unfolding of those fears in their own time—not ours.

"There's just too much going on today. I really don't have time for this!"

We all have all the time in the world. It's just a matter of how we choose to use it.

Doubt:

"What if I never experience God? What if all of this is a lie?"

Do you hold a belief about what you feel God is or should be held up against your experiences? If so, you've already set yourself up for failure. We don't believe when we see, but rather see when we believe. Faith and trust are our companions as the mystery informs us.

"I doubt if a spiritual practice will really make a difference in my life. I've just got to deal with what I've been handed."

It's never so much about what we've been handed as how we chose to be with what we've been handed. Two people having had very similar experiences may find one lost in despair and the other, also in despair, transforming

Part 3: Singing the Holy

the seemingly unforgivable to heal themselves and, sometimes, others as well.

"Who says this stuff works anyway? I want proof, or at least a guarantee, before I devote my good time to this."

If, before starting, you require proof, you'll never get to know what awaits in your inner wilderness and discover that joy that comes in the morning.

CONCLUSION

What Lovers Know

*Listen to the wind, it talks. Listen to the silence,
it speaks. Listen to your heart, it knows.*[1]

NATIVE AMERICAN PROVERB

A COMMON CHRISTIAN WISDOM emphasizes Jesus' teaching that we must be born again to have a new realization of to whom it is we belong. The early disciples and followers of Jesus experienced what has been called the ecstatic cry of joy—the joy that comes from a full, direct *experience* of the Christ. Similarly, in the Bhagavad Gita, Krishna, the divine personified, tells Arjuna that in order to succeed on the battlefield of life he must hand over the reins of his chariot to him—to keep his mind single-pointed, his heart devoted, to offer his actions up, and to bow his ego down.[2] It's in this way that he too may remember to whom it is he belongs and have a direct experience of the divine. And just like the early Christian disciples and Arjuna, we too can realize, through direct experience, to whom it is we belong and find ourselves, more often, proclaiming that involuntarily ecstatic cry of joy.

This direct experience of the divine is exactly what we're offered when we become lovers in the Sonic Trilogy of Love and brave

1. Goodreads, "Listen," para. 2.
2. Satchidananda, *Living Gita*, 295.

our inner wilderness in our Mantra Prayer practice. But—and this may surprise you—ultimately it's not particularly important what happens in our practice as we begin to encounter those moments of joyful mystical unity. What's infinitely more important is what happens when we leave our practice and walk out into our life. It's there that we discover that we naturally begin to carry and share that joy, that devotional joy not hinged on circumstance, to enliven all around us. Graciously and wondrously, in the end, we get to finally discover it was never about *us* at all. And *this* becomes *the* greatest gift.

So, in conclusion, let's highlight some of the guidelines we've discussed that will help us, as lovers, to *be* that love everlasting in our daily walk.

PRACTICE RADICAL SELF-ACCEPTANCE

The first challenge is to be, fully, *with what is.* We can't transform and release into a new awareness of anything we're not willing to fully embrace. And we can rest assured that the awareness, healing, and release we're seeking is just on the other side of our deep resistance. This is why Meister Eckhart said, "It is in the darkness that one finds the light."[3] So, he reminds us, it is actually when we are in our deepest sorrow that the light is nearest of all to us. Often when the mind is conjuring up boredom or doubt or when there's a persistent restlessness, the mental defenses or obstacles are working hard to protect us from the next level of awareness ready to surface. And, as we've seen, the deeper the resistance, the more profound the hidden awareness. Persevere. Tune. New songs are yearning to be sung.

It's quite an amazing process to discover that simply by being *with what is,* the ties that bind slowly loosen. Something we may have struggled with for a very long time can simply dissolve when held open in the kiln of our compassionate heart. And, often, we're left wondering why, oh why, we held on, suffered, for so long when freedom was so close. It's okay. We first have to be willing to step off the ledge before we can discover we can fly. We must have

---

3. McGinn, *Meister Eckhart*, 147.

the courage to face our deepest fears in order to discover they are simply illusions our mind has adopted as truth. And, when we do, and we witness the dissipating and deep release of something we truly believed would be with us forever, we find ourselves resting and silent in the soft hand of God.

SIT AT THE FEET OF YOUR LIFE TO BE TAUGHT

Polly Berrien Berends said, "Everything that happens to you is your teacher. The secret is to learn to sit at the feet of your own life and be taught by it."[4] She and others have reflected the great truth that everything that happens is either a blessing which is also a lesson, or a lesson which is also a blessing. Earth has been called a kind of schoolhouse for souls, and this sentiment is echoed across many traditions. The notion of sitting at the feet of our life to be taught also provides a kind of distance needed to remember that we're only here to do our part, to play a role. It's one of those spiritual paradoxes that all must be felt completely in order to receive the deeper lessons, and, yet, it's equally important to remember that in the role we play, all experience, the challenging as well as the delightful, will pass. As Swami Satchidananda said in *The Living Gita*, "The first lesson is to know that everything is here to test you; don't be deceived by it. Pass the test. Don't hate the examiner; love him."[5] Let's work on being good students so we can soon graduate!

I think of every experience as my teacher, most especially the difficult ones. It's helpful to remember that right when I'm in the thick of suffering, I know something good is going to come of it. This *good* does not necessarily refer to an emotion. Rather, the newfound awareness may be *good* while, indeed, the overall experience needed to bring the awareness may be, necessarily, extremely challenging and difficult. I believe this is the role of suffering. Suffering cracks us open to allow for the light. Yet, we can choose to accept the light or hide under our bushel, as the well-known song "This

---

4. https://www.goodreads.com/author/quotes/110396.Polly_Berrien_Berends.

5. Satchidananda, *Living Gita*, 243.

Little Light of Mine" reminds us. The challenge is not to avert the emotional landscape along the way but, rather, to fully embrace it. Embracing the emotions allows for a clearing, a kind of calm after the storm, to occur, during which we can more clearly receive the deeper lessons of our experience.

REMEMBER WHO YOU ARE

And as our Mantra Prayer practice is busy clearing away all that stands in the way of the fullest experience of our inner divinity and is also creating new neural pathways for expanded awareness and experience, its most important job is preparing the conditions so we may hear in the silence that follows—experience those unforeseen moments of mystical unity with our beloved God. And once we've experienced such a moment—love's kiss—nothing is the same. We *know* now that we're not just a drop in the ocean but are made of the very essence of the ocean itself—made in the image and likeness of God (see Gen 1:27)—and that every other person and part of God's creation is also. We *know* now, not just believe, that we're one with all, that we live in the heart of God.

And this knowing brings that joy, that devotional joy, not predicated on outside circumstance, No, this joy eternally springs from the still point resting in our center, the ultimate expression of who we truly are, a beacon of light that can sustain us through all of life's storms and seasons. We can clearly see now that this joy is different from simply practicing the power of positive thinking. This joy isn't just another mind state. Rather, it naturally comes *through* the mind into our experience when the mind is held in equanimity. It's why the Buddha said, "To enjoy good health, to bring true happiness to one's family, to bring peace to all, one must discipline and control one's own mind. If a man can control his mind, he can find the way to enlightenment and all wisdom and virtue will naturally come to him."[6]

---

6. https://www.brainyquote.com/quotes/buddha_118245.

Conclusion: What Lovers Know

CHOOSE JOY!

As we practice radical self-acceptance sitting at the feet of our life to be taught and allow for all of our human journey to move through, leaving only the imprints of the valuable lessons learned, we begin, more often, to know the joy that does, indeed, come in the morning (see Ps 30:5). Slowly, we realize that we can choose this joy when there's a remembrance that all of life is unfolding perfectly and is, in fact, all quite good, even when it may not seem or feel that way. We get less rattled less often. Less and less we need life to be good to be happy.

For now, we've become lovers. We've stepped into the Sonic Trilogy of Love to brave our inner wilderness. Using the love in the sacred sound currents of our Mantra Prayer practice we continue to release what stands in the way of experiencing our innate divinity even as we cultivate new, more helpful mind states allowing for healing, forgiveness, courage, focus, and abundance. And, along the way, we've learned how to create an inner space for our beloved's visit and for, graciously, those sweet moments of mystical unity, love's kiss, that change everything.

And we are glad.

APPENDIX A

Sample Mantra Prayers from Six Faith Traditions

Judaism, Christianity, Sufism, Hinduism, Buddhism, and Sikhism

I'VE BEEN EXTREMELY BLESSED to have been able to spend many years experiencing mantra practices from a variety of faith traditions. Included here is just a small sampling of the practices with which I have worked. They're offered simply as a starting place for those of you not already familiar with mantra practice. There are, of course, literally thousands of mantra, and if you are already devoted to a lineage of practices from a particular faith tradition, you may or may not be drawn to incorporate any of the practices below. Use as best fits your needs!

Offered here are breath practices and mantra meditations from the following faith traditions: Judaism, Christianity, Sufism, Hinduism, Buddhism, and Sikhism. It's important to note that in order to truly receive the most from any particular practice, it's very helpful to have the guidance of a teacher or guide from the faith tradition representing the practice you are undertaking.

When you are ready to choose a particular mantra for your Mantra Prayer practice, you'll see that I have numbered each

Appendix A

mantra indicating the quality or qualities for which each is largely known. This may be helpful to you when choosing to create a practice specifically for healing, forgiveness, courage, focus, or abundance. These practice intentions and their numbers are: healing (1); forgiveness (2); courage (3); focus (4); and abundance (5).

Finally, I have offered the source for the information presented for each mantra so you can explore further if so desired and have also offered my personal reflections in the "Author's Note" section of each mantra practice presented. You can find all of the mantra in audio form on my website: https://www.stephanierutt.com/ under "Book Audios."

JUDAISM

Breath Practice

Breathing Chedvah: Breathing Joy

Chedvah means joy. This joy has been described as the sharp, first initial experience of joy. Breathing *chedvah* means to breathe this joy into our souls and bodies. This happens in a repeating cycle of inhaling, holding, exhaling, and resting.

Inhale: 1–8 counts
    Inhaling means to aspire.
Hold: 4 counts
    Holding brings the super conscious experience into the beginning of consciousness.
Exhale: 6 counts
    Exhaling brings the consciousness into the body.
Rest: 5 counts
    Resting, also known as the Mother Principle, means consciousness has reached its place, destination, and resonates there.

The cycle of 8-4-6-5 corresponds to the Hebrew script numerical values spelling of *chedvah*.

Source: Gal Einai Institute; Rabbi Yitzchak Ginsburgh. What is offered here is the basic breathing practice. You're invited to visit https://www.inner.org/homepage/chedvah-breathing-method[1] for much more information on this important breath practice.

1. Ginsburgh, "Chedvah," lines 1–4.

Appendix A

Author's Note: You'll find this breath opens us to the fullness of joy within, that joy of eternal devotion.

Mantra Prayers

Shema Yisrael Adonai Eloheynu Adonai Echad (1,2,3,4,5)

Shema—listen with every fiber of your being
Yisrael—all who wrestle with God
Adonai—the Lord
Eloheynu—our God
Echad—is One
Repeat as desired.
This well-loved Jewish chant is from Deuteronomy 6:4 and is arguably the most cherished phrase in the entire Hebrew Bible. It contains two important affirmations: that *Adonai* is *our* God, not simply remote and abstract; and that *Adonai* is One. The words form the beginning of the *Shema*, the central prayer in the Jewish prayerbook, the *Siddur*. It is often the first section of Scripture that a Jewish child learns, and many Jews recite the *Shema* twice daily, once in the morning and once in the evening.

Source: Siddur Eit Ratzon[2]

Author's Note: Chanting this mantra invites us to walk in the footsteps of Moses. Here we find humanity and humility as well as profound faith and trust.

Ahava Raba Ahavtanu (5)

Ahava Raba—[with an] abundant or great love
Ahavtanu—you have loved us
Repeat as desired.
This is the last blessing preceding the *Shema* offered above and speaks of God as the One who loves the Jewish people. The full prayer describes three ways in which this love is manifested: through compassion, guidance, and presence.

Source: Siddur Eit Ratzon[3]

2. Rosenstein, *Siddur*, 51.
3. Rosenstein, *Siddur*, 49.

Sample Mantra Prayers from Six Faith Traditions

Author's Note: This mantra reminds us of how great and magnificent is God's love. We don't have to strive to be worthy of this love. All we need do is simply collapse into the arms of the beloved as all that stands between us and our creator is transformed.

Kadosh Kadosh Kadosh Adonai Elohim Tz' Va' Ot (1,5)

Kadosh—holy
Adonai—our Lord
Elohim—our God
Tz' Va' Ot—Lord of Hosts
Repeat as desired.

This mantra is found in the third part of the *Amidah*, the Standing Prayer, which is the core prayer of every Jewish service. It is built around three verses. In Isaiah's vision (Isa 6:3), the angels proclaim God's holiness and declare that God's presence fills the world, themes echoed in Ezekiel's vision (Ezek 3:12). This declaration of God's spiritual presence, of God's holiness, is followed by Psalm 146:10, a declaration of God's material presence, of God's rulership.

Source: Siddur Eit Ratzon[4]

Author's Note: Chanting this mantra elicits a sweet devotion, opening the heart to engage directly with the holiness within.

Adonai Roee Lo Echsar (4,5)

Adonai—the Lord
Roee—my Shepherd
Lo—not
Echsar—will I lack
Repeat as desired.

Source: Shalom Scripture Studies, Inc.[5]

Author's Note: It's interesting to notice that the Hebrew translation is not "The Lord is my Shepherd. I shall not want." Rather, the second line translates "not will I lack." This is a beautiful reminder that we are, indeed, already full. We may still desire and enjoy many things but not from a sense of lacking.

---

4. Rosenstein, *Siddur*, 61.
5. Molloy, "Psalm 23."

Appendix A

A Psalm of David: Psalm 23 (1,2,3,4,5)

Translation and transliteration of the Hebrew: Reading from right to left:

ECHSAR LO ROEE	ADONAI	L'DAVID	MIZMOR
ek sar low rowee	*Ah doh n eye*	*La'Day veed*	*Mees more*
will I lack not	my shepherd	The Lord	of David A Psalm

The Lord is my shepherd; I shall not want.

YARBITZEINI	DESHE	BINOT
yar beet say knee	*dea shea*	*bean ote*
He makes me lie down	tender grass	in pastures

He makes me lie down in green pastures:

Y'NAHALEINI	MENUCHOT	AL-MEI
ya nah hah lay knee	*men oh hote*	*all-may*
He leadeth me	the still	beside waters

he leads me beside the still waters.

V'MAGLEI	YANCHEINI	Y'SHOVEIV	NAFSHI
vah mah ah glaa	*yahn hi knee*	*ye show veil*	*nauf she*
in the paths	He guides me	He restoreth	my soul

He restores my soul: he leads me in the paths

SH'MO	L'MAN	TZEDEK
sh' moe	*lay 'mah aun*	*zaa dick*
his name's	for sake	righteousness

of righteousness for his name's sake.

TZALMAVET	B'GEL	KI-EILEICH	GAM
zaul mah vet	*be'gates*	*key ee let*	*gaum*
the shadow of death	in the valley	am walking	When

Yea, though I walk through the valley of the shadow of death,

EMADI	KI-ATA	RO	EIRA -	LO
ee mah dee	*kee-ah tah*	*rah*	*era -*	*low*
with me	you are	for evil	will I fear -	no

I will fear no evil for thou art with me;

Y'NACHAMUNI	HEMA	U'MISHANTECHA	SHIVTECHA
ya' nah who moe nee	*heamah*	*u' me shaun tecka*	*sheev tecka*
comfort me	they	and your staff	your rod

thy rod and thy staff they comfort me.

Sample Mantra Prayers from Six Faith Traditions

TZOR'RAI	NEGED	SHULCHAN	L'FANAI	TAAROCKH
zor row eye	*neh get*	*shul haun*	*lea'fana*	*tah ah roak*
mine enemies	before	table	before me	You prepare

Thou preparest a table before me in the presence of mine enemies:

R'VAYA	KOSI	ROSHI	V'SHEMEN	DISHANTA
rev'vah ya	*kos ee*	*row she*	*vah'shea men*	*dee shaunta*
runs over	my cup	my head	with oil	you anointed

thou anointest my head with oil; my cup runneth over.

YIRD'FUNI	VA'CHESED	TOV	ACH
yard'funi	*vah eck said*	*tow*	*ack*
shall follow me	and mercy	goodness	Surely

Surely goodness and mercy shall follow me

V'SHAVTI	CHAYYAI	KOL-Y'MEI
vay'shauv tee	*hi yigh*	*koal-ee' ya may*
and I shall dwell	my life	the days of all

all the days of my life and I shall dwell

YAMIN	L'ORECH	ADONAI	-	B'BEIT
yah mean	*lay'oh reck*	*Ah doe n eye*	-	*bee bet*
days	for the length of	the Lord	-	in the house

in the house of the Lord forever.
Amen

Source: Both the translation from Hebrew as well as the presentation of the Psalm is used here with permission from: Shalom Scripture Studies, Inc.[6] *The English transliteration is my added creation.*

Author's Note: Though a lengthy practice, I cannot recommend it highly enough.

---

6. Molloy, "Psalm 23."

Appendix A

CHRISTIANITY

Breath Practice

Abba: I Belong to You

From Rom 8:15, "For you did not receive a spirit of slavery to fall back into fear, but you received a spirit of adoption. When we cry, 'Abba! Father!'"
Repeat as desired.
This breath practice was originated by Brennan Manning who invited us to simply breathe in *Abba* and breathe out *I belong to you*. Manning said, "Define yourself radically as one beloved by God. This is the true self. Every other identity is illusion."

Source: Brennan Manning's *A Furious Longing for God*.[7] You can find out more about him at www.brennanmanning.com.

Author's Note: This simple breath is a profound practice when we remember, that with each breath, we are proclaiming that we did not receive a spirit of fear but the spirit of adoption. This powerful phrase may also be used as a mantra practice if so desired.

---

7. Manning, *Furious Longing for God*, 46–47.

Sample Mantra Prayers from Six Faith Traditions

Mantra Prayers

Om Jesu Christaya Paramatmane Purusha Avataraya Namaha (4,5)

Om—universal creative sound
Jesu Christaya—Jesus Christ
Paramatmane—presiding soul of all souls
Purusha—Divine Oversoul
Avataraya—world teacher
Repeat 108+ times.
This mantra is said in praise of Jesus. The translation reminds us that Jesus is a world teacher, *Avataraya*, and carries the authority of the Divine transcendental, *Purusha*, or God.

Source: *Healing Mantras*[8]

Author's Note: This mantra is a wonderful way to align with the spirit of Jesus to receive the true message in the teachings of this one called a presiding soul of all souls.

Sixth Beatitude: Blessed are the pure in heart: for they will see God (1,2,3,4,5)

Tubwayhun layleyn dadkeyn b'lebhon d'hinnon nehzun l'alah

Tubwayhun—blessed.
layleyn—to those; roots go back to an image of one watching by night, waiting by lamplight for something to happen, a kind of desire that creates a vortex of possibility that draws in the object of the heart.
dadkeyn—refers to those consistent in love or sympathy, those who have both a natural sense of influence and abundance and a fixed, electrifying purpose. The old roots call up the image of a flower blossoming because that is its nature.
b'lebhon—translated as "heart" and also carries the sense of any center from which life radiates, a sense of expansion plus generative power: vitality, desire, affection, courage, and audacity all rolled into one.

---

8. Ashely-Farrand, *Healing Mantras*, 185.

Appendix A

d'hinnon—referring to those who are pure in heart.
nehzun—translated as "see" but also points to inner vision or contemplation. The old roots evoke the image of a flash of lightning that appears suddenly in the sky: the way insight comes.
l'ahaha—God or the One. The roots point to the force and passionate movement of the cosmos through the soul of every living thing.
Repeat as desired.

Source: Matt 5:8, Aramaic translation from *Prayers of the Cosmos*[9]

Author's Note: This beatitude is considered a key teaching in the Sermon on the Mount, and chanting it truly quickens a remembrance that if we can be pure of heart, we too shall see God. With commitment to our daily practice, we can cultivate new eyes to see, new ears to hear, and a new heart to know.

Ave Maria, Gratia Plena (3,4,5)

Ave Maria—Hail Mary
Gratia Plena—Full of Grace
Repeat as desired.

Source: Luke 1:28, "And he came to her and said, 'Greetings, favored one! The Lord is with you.'" The mantra uses the words of the angel Gabriel when he announced to Mary that she was to bear the Christ child. NRSV.

Author's Note: Invite yourself into the realization that, as Christian mystic Meister Eckhart said, "We are all meant to be mothers of God . . . for God is always needing to be born."[10] This happens, ultimately, when we are able to fully align our will with Divine will to bring forth our unique purpose in creation.

Lord's Prayer Opening Line: Awoon dwashmaya (4,5)

Awoon—derived from *Abba* (see *Abba: I Belong to You* breath practice at the beginning of this section on Christian practices) referring to an almost childlike "daddy" or "papa," conjuring up feelings of an intimate, loving, and compassionate presence. When we call God "Father," we acknowledge our kinship with him as we would a parent.

---

9. Douglas-Klotz, *Prayers*, 62–63.

10. https://www.goodreads.com/quotes/439121-we-are-all-meant-to-be-mothers-of-god-for-god.

dwashmaya—means *who is in heaven* (in the Aramaic text the verb "is" is not present).
Repeat as desired.

Source: Setting a Trap for God[11]

Author's Note: When the disciples of Jesus asked how they should pray, Jesus answered with reciting what was to be called The Lord's Prayer. Believed to have spoken in Aramaic, Jesus would have begun by saying "Awoon dwashmaya," commonly interpreted from the Greek as "Our Father which art in Heaven." However, translating and examining the opening phrase through the lens of the Aramaic language, new and expanded meanings are revealed. "Awoon" stirs a memory of what exists eternally beyond, yet fully supporting, our daily experience. "Dwashmaya" reveals the entire manifested world as we experience through our senses or what makes the eternal aspect knowable. So, in chanting this phrase in Aramaic, we are connecting our eternal soul with the experience of our daily human journey in the world of manifestation. We become whole.

---

11. Errico, *Setting a Trap*, 27–39.

Appendix A

The Lord's Prayer (1,2,3,4,5)

General Aramaic Interpretations in Bold Italics	Aramaic Transliterations in Parentheses
Our Father which art in heaven, *Remember...*	Abwoon d'bwashmaya, (Ah **bwoon** deh'baush **maya**)
Hallowed be thy name. *Create Space...*	Nethqadash shmakh. (net **kau** dish shm*uck*)
Thy kingdom come. *Align with the Creator...*	Teytey malkuthakh. (taa taa **maul** koo *tah*)
Thy will be done *Manifest the Vision...*	Nehwey tzevyanach aykanna (*ne*whay se bee ya*na* ikana)
in earth, as it is in heaven. *Become Heaven on Earth...*	d'bwashmaya, aph b'arha. (deh'baush **maya off** bah'are **ahhhh**)
Give us this day our daily bread. *Embrace Fullness...*	Hawvlan lachma d'sunqanan yaomana. (**hauv** laun **lock** mah d'soon kau nan yah oh **mana**)
And forgive us our debts (trespasses), *Forgive Self...*	Washboqlan khaubayn (wakhtahayn), (**wash** bah **claun** *how* **bain** *walk* tau **hain**)
as we forgive our debtors (trespassers) *Forgive Others...*	aykanna daph khnan shbwoqan (wakhtahayn) (ikana *duf* **kahnan** *shwa* kau nal' **hi** ya bain)
And lead us not into temptation, *Resist Forgetfulness...*	Wela tahlan l'nesyuna, (**way lah** *tau* laun **leh'**neh **suna**)
but deliver us from evil: *Cultivate Harmony...*	ela patzan min bisha: (**aa** lah patzan men **bee** sha)
For thine is the kingdom, *For Thine is the Vision...*	Metol dilakhie malkuthakh, (meh tool deh *lahk* hay **maul** koo *tah*)
and the power, and the glory, *the Energy...and the Song...*	wahayla, wateshbukhta, (*wah* **hi** lah wah tesh **book** tah)
forever. *forever.*	l'ahlam almin. (l'ah**laum** al**mean**)
Amen. *Amen.*	Ameyn. (ah **main**)

Source: *The Aramaic translation in the right column is from Prayers of the Cosmos.*[12] *Note that Neil Douglas-Klotz's spelling of the opening line, "Abwoon d'bwashmaya," is slightly different from Rocco A. Errico's rendering of the line in the previous practice, "Awoon dwashmaya." Both the transliteration in the right column as well as the general Aramaic interpretation in the left column are mine.*

12. Douglas-Klotz, *Prayers*, 10–41.

Sample Mantra Prayers from Six Faith Traditions

Author's Note: The reader is invited to reference the author's book, Living the Prayer of Jesus: A Study of the Lord's Prayer in Aramaic *(Wipf & Stock Publishers, 2019), available on Amazon, for a complete study of the prayer. Reciting the Lord's Prayer in Aramaic opens awareness to the inner teachings of the prayer in ways that are difficult to articulate. For many, it has birthed a new devotion to the prayer specifically and to the teachings of Jesus in general.*

SUFISM

Note: I had the great blessing to learn and experience the breath and mantra, or sacred phrase, practices offered here during several years of study at SAMA, Center of Sufi Ruhaniat International, in Cambridge, Massachusetts. The Ruhaniat is a branch of Universal Sufism stemming from Hazrat Inayat Khan and Murshid Samuel Lewis who founded the Dances of Universal Peace.

Breath Practices

Breath of Light

On the "in" breath mentally repeat *Ya Rassoul*
On the "out" breath mentally repeat *Ya Makboul*
Ya Rassoul—Breathe in blessings of light from the whole universe.
Ya Makboul—Breathe out the feeling of your own light being an expression of that light.
Practice 10+ minutes.

Source: Esoteric Teachings from the Sufi Ruhaniat International

Appendix A

Author's Note: This is a simple and beautiful breath practice that instantly reminds us that we are made of light yet, much like different colored light bulbs, we each have our own unique expression of that light.

Purification Breaths

Preferably, begin standing and proceed in a relaxed and unconstrained manner.
Inhale–Exhale through the nose 5 times
Inhale through the nose–Exhale through the mouth 5 times
Inhale through the mouth–Exhale through the nose 5 times
Inhale–Exhale through the mouth 5 times
Inhale–Exhale through the nose 5 times, imagining all of your pores and cells are breathing, cleansing, and healing.
Repeat as desired.

Source: Esoteric Teachings the Sufi Ruhaniat International

Author's Note: This is one of the few breath practices that, ideally, is practiced standing. You will find this adds an important dimension as it teaches us to "practice relaxing where we stand."

Healing Breaths (with Sacred Phrase)

Ya Shafee—O Healer
Ya Kaffee—O Remedy
As you inhale, mentally repeat *Ya Shafee*.
As you exhale, mentally repeat *Ya Kaffee*.
Practice 10+ minutes.

Source: Esoteric Teachings from the Sufi Ruhaniat International

Author's Note: This powerful healing breath engages our mental energies to support a remembrance that the beloved is in each breath we take as both healer and remedy. How wonderful to know that healing is only a breath away.

Sample Mantra Prayers from Six Faith Traditions

Sacred Phrases

Those familiar with Islamic and Sufi practices will recognize the sacred phrases below as some of the ninety-nine Beautiful Names of God recorded in the Qur'an. I present them here, in pairs, as I learned them in my esoteric studies with the Sufi Ruhaniat International.

Ya Ahad Ya Samad (4,5)

For this practice, it is helpful to use a visual image of a dot in the center of a circle.
Ya Ahad—"The One" (illustrated by the "dot")
The dot symbolizes the unique, mysterious you—the place in your heart that is so precious to you that you alone can feel it, sense it, embody it.
Ya Samad—"The Infinite" (illustrated by the "circle")
The circle symbolizes the infinite place of refuge that engulfs us when we fall into the heart of God, live in the heart of God, and surrender to the mystery that is us.
Suggestion: Create your own image of a dot in the center of a circle. Meditate on the image as you repeat *Ya Ahad Ya Samad* 101+ times.

Source: *Esoteric Teachings from the Sufi Ruhaniat International and The Sufi Book of Life*[13]

Author's Note: *When I introduce this practice, I often describe the "dot" as the embodiment of our soul's purpose and the surrounding "circle" as all the forces of the universe that are there, just waiting, to support our walk when we dare to embrace our true calling.*

Ya Qadir, Ya Muqtadir (3,4,5)

Ya Qadir—"Holding the Center"
Ya Qadir reminds us that everything in the universe is connected by the Divine Strength of the One and awakens us to this unlimited Power enabling us to both manifest and contain manifestation. Invocation of *Ya Qadir* is an antidote to feeling worthless or powerless and to the belief that one is living a wasted life.

13. Douglas-Klotz, *Sufi Book*, 184; 186.

Appendix A

Ya Muqtadir—"Embodying Power in Action"
Ya Muqtadir is the One who places us on a particular path to God, enables us to firmly put our feet on that path, and supports us to keep going on that path, step by step, by placing one foot in front of the other. *Ya Muqtadir* brings the ability to actualize our Divine Purpose.
Repeat *Ya Qadir Ya Muqtadir* 101+ times.

Source: Esoteric Teachings from the Sufi Ruhaniat International and The Sufi Book of Life[14]

Author's Note: This practice is wonderful for those who are in search of what their true purpose might be. It enables an inner cultivation of inner power so that personal will may be in service to divine will.

Ya Wasi Ya Wali (1,3,5)

Ya Wasi—"Limitless Expansive Capacity"
Ya Wasi invites us to expand the capacity of the heart to hold and embrace whatever may come into our orbit. Here we remember that we are never alone and that we can be present for any circumstance when our heart is fully open and expansive.
Ya Wali—"The Nearest Friend"
Ya Wali reminds us that there is no sweeter or more intimate friend than the beloved.
Repeat *Ya Wasi Ya Wali* 101+ times.

Source: Esoteric Teachings from the Sufi Ruhaniat International and The Sufi Book of Life[15]

Author's Note: This practice is the antidote to the core fear that we are alone. It reminds us that, no matter what may come into our experience, we can turn to our inner Beloved who is, indeed, our closest, sweetest, most intimate friend.

Ya Ra'uf Ya Rahim (1,2,3,5)

Ya Ra'uf—"Healing Love"
Ya Ra'uf specifically addresses past wounds we've received from family or humanity. It evokes a sense of resting in God in the midst of fear, hostility, and struggle.

14. Douglas-Klotz, *Sufi Book*, 189; 192.
15. Douglas-Klotz, *Sufi Book*, 122; 150.

Sample Mantra Prayers from Six Faith Traditions

Ya Rahim—"The Moon of Love"
Ya Rahim evokes a sense of compassionate receptivity. Reciting *Ya Rahim* opens us to receive love and compassion wherever we need it most.
Repeat *Ya Ra'uf Ya Rahim* 101+ times.

Source: Esoteric Teachings from the Sufi Ruhaniat International and *The Sufi Book of Life*[16]

Author's Note: This is a deeply healing practice that transforms the most profound hurts and feelings of injustice. It makes good compost of our hurts so we may begin to imagine growing new awareness and possibilities.

Ya Ghaffar Ya Ghafour; Ya Tawwab Ya Afuw (1,2,4,5)

Ya Ghaffar—"The Pardoner"
Ya Ghaffar calls out to divine forgiveness, particularly for that mistake we make over and over again, to burn away tension and hurt.
Ya Ghafour—"The Forgiver—The Forgiveness of Light"
Ya Ghafour calls out to divine forgiveness to penetrate to the depths of our hearts with light, particularly to that which we find unforgiveable.
Ya Ghaffar and *Ya Ghafour* have been described as repairing cracks in the dried out leather water carrier, bringing suppleness back into our life. It is important to remember that forgiveness is a process whereby we soften our own heart to heal those places inside of ourselves where we hold hurt, anger, judgment, and criticism. Repeat *Ya Ghaffar Ya Ghafour* 101+ times.
Ya Tawwab—"The Repenter"
With *Ya Tawwab*, we turn away from the fault to face God—and there we find God looking at us.
Ya Afuw—"The Forgiver—Blowing Away the Ashes"
At this stage of forgiveness, we completely let go of the fault. The wind has completely erased the tracks in the sand. Repeat *Ya Ghaffar Ya Ghafour; Ya Tawwab Ya Afuw* 101+ times.

---

16. Douglas-Klotz, *Sufi Book*, 228; 9.

Appendix A

Source: Esoteric Teachings from the Sufi Ruhaniat International and The Sufi Book of Life[17]

Author's Note: I usually recommend that Ya Ghaffar and Ya Ghafour be taken on as a practice for at least forty days before adding Ya Tawwab Ya Afuw. This is a profound practice for forgiveness that unfolds and heals us in stages. Let's honor each stage as it's revealed allowing spaciousness for the deepest emotions to emerge. Peace is waiting at the journey's end.

---

17. Douglas-Klotz, *Sufi Book*, 39; 92; 221; 226.

HINDUISM

Breath Practices

Three-Part Diaphragmatic Breath

If you are not familiar with diaphragmatic breathing, you may want to first practice this breath lying on your back. If you are familiar with the breathing, you can practice while sitting.

Begin by relaxing with some soft deep breaths. Allow your exhale to be slightly longer than your inhale as you relax more deeply. Place one hand over your abdomen and the other over the center of your chest. Imagine in your mind's eye a picture of your lungs, how they expand at the bottom and become narrow towards the top. Now, soften your belly as you imagine filling your lungs from the bottom up. This softening of the belly allows for the diaphragm to drop down so the lower lungs can fill with breath. Feel your hand over your abdomen rise as you soften your belly and fill the lower lungs with breath. Imagine continuing to fill your lungs until your other hand over your chest also rises. On the exhale, imagine releasing the breath from the top down so the hand over your chest first relaxes down followed by the hand over your abdomen.

You will notice that the continuous movement creates a kind of "wave" of breath. This is how babies naturally breathe and how we are designed to breathe. Once you have mastered the breath while lying down, practice sitting up. As you practice, your body will naturally

Appendix A

remember this innate flow and new levels of calm and peace will permeate your being.

Author's Note: The above is a composite of many writings on the Three-Part Diaphragmatic Breath I used during the years I taught yoga. This fundamental breathing practice changes how we feel in our bodies and, as a result, how we feel in our daily life.

Mantra Prayers

Om Sri Rama Jaya Rama Jaya Jaya Rama (1,3,5)

Om—universal creative sound or primordial sound (The most basic mantra is *Aum*, which in Hinduism is known as the *"pranava* mantra," the source of all mantra.)
Sri—divine feminine
Rama—seventh Avatar of Vishnu
Jaya—victory
This mantra is called the Taraka or Liberation Mantra and will eventually burn off all karma. It helps to achieve spiritual freedom by reducing and eliminating lust, anger, and fear.
Repeat 108+ times.

Source: Teacher of Mantra Instruction Manual[18]

Author's Note: Taraka could be loosely defined as one that helps us cross, cross over the cycles of birth and death. This mantra was chanted regularly by Mahatma Gandhi.

Om Shrim Maha Lakshmiyae Swaha (5)

Om—universal creative sound
Shrim—seed sound for attracting abundance
Maha—"much" abundance!
Lakshmiyae—presiding deity over the principle of abundance
Swaha—salutation/invocation at the solar plexus chakra

---

18. Ashley-Farrand, *Teacher of Mantra*, 122.

Sample Mantra Prayers from Six Faith Traditions

Lakshmi is the source for spiritual abundance, health, inner peace, financial wealth, friendship, the love of children, and family.
This is a powerful mantra for attracting abundance in many forms.
Repeat 108+ times.

Source: *Healing Mantras*[19]

Author's Note: This is a well-known mantra practice for attracting financial abundance in particular. If we offer our efforts in service to a greater good then, of course, we will be provided with all we need to manifest our divine purpose!

Om Hram Hirayna Gharbhaya Namaha (1)

Om—universal creative sound
Hram—seed sound
Hirayna Gharbhaya—golden colored one (healing gold)
Namaha—salutation/invocation
This mantra brings healing energy in the form of golden light from the sun to heal the one afflicted.
Repeat 108+ times.

Source: *Healing Mantras*[20]

Author's Note: As you chant this mantra, visualize healing golden light coming to any place in your body you may feel the need.

Om Gam Ganapatayee Namaha (1,3)

Om—universal creative sound
Gam—seed sound for the removal of obstacles
Gunapati—another word for Ganesha
Yei—shakti activating sound
Namaha—salutation/invocation
This mantra is used to remove obstacles even if you don't know what the specific obstacle may be.
Repeat 108+ times.

Source: *Teacher of Mantra Instruction Manual*[21]

---

19. Ashley-Farrand, *Healing Mantras*, 63.
20. Ashley-Farrand, *Healing Mantras*, 116.
21. Ashley-Farrand, *Teacher of Mantra*, 209.

Appendix A

Author's Note: Sometimes obstacles are there for a reason and bring their own gifts if explored more deeply. I would not recommend using this mantra to just get rid of something uncomfortable but rather to remove unnecessary obstacles to a specific goal or desire.

The Chamundi Mantra: Om Eim Hrim Klim Chamundayae Vich'chae Namaha (3)

Om—universal creative sound
Eim—seed sound for Saraswati—presiding over sound, arts, and sciences both material and spiritual—and she also helps to dispel negative energy.
Hrim—seed sound for seeing through the illusions of our experience.
Klim—seed sound for the principle of attraction.
Chamundi—the beautiful aspect of the feminine that, nonetheless, can be utterly destructive to a wide variety of negative forces.
Yae—shakti activating sound
Vich'chae—to cut through
Namaha—salutation/invocation
The Chamundi Mantra is a mantra for the feminine principle of Devi as the power of protection. This mantra is said to produce tangible power and the wisdom to use it properly. It provides proactive protection and the destruction of negative forces or entities. Prolonged use has been reported to produce feelings of self-confidence or self-esteem, especially in women.
Repeat 108+ times.

Source: *Teacher of Mantra Instruction Manual*[22]

Author's Note: This mantra has a great cadence making it very easy to learn, maintain, and enjoy in practice.

The Gayatri Mantra—Known as the "Mother" of all Mantra (1,2,3,4,5)

There are two forms of this mantra, the long and the short form. The short form is practiced by the vast majority of those who chant this mantra. I will give you both forms.

---

22. Ashley-Farrand, *Teacher of Mantra*, 190.

Sample Mantra Prayers from Six Faith Traditions

Long Form:	Short Form:
Om Bhu Om Bhuvaha Om Swaha	Om Bhur Bhuvaha Swaha
Om Maha Om Janaha Om Tapaha Om Satyam	
Om Tat Savitur Varenyam	Om Tat Savitur Varenyam
Bhargo Devasya Dhimahi	Bhargo Devasya Dhimahi
Dhiyo Yonaha Prachodayat	Dhiyo Yonaha Prachodayat

Om Bhu—earth plane (first chakra)
Om Bhuvaha—atmospheric plane (second chakra)
Om Swaha—solar region (third chakra)
Om Maha—first spiritual region beyond the sun; heart vibration (fourth chakra)
Om Janaha—second spiritual region beyond the sun; throat vibration—power of the divine spiritual word (fifth chakra)
Om Tapaha—third spiritual region beyond the sun; sphere of the progenitors (sixth chakra)—represents the highest realm of spiritual understanding one can attain while still identified with individual existence
Om Satyam—the abode of supreme Truth; absorption into the Supreme (seventh chakra)
Om Tat Savitur Varenyam—the realm of Truth that is beyond human comprehension
Bhargo Devasya Dhimahi—in that place where all the celestials of all the spheres have received enlightenment
Dhiyo Yonaha Prachodayat—kindly enlighten our intellect
Repeat 108+ times.

Source: *Teacher of Mantra Instruction Manual*[23]

Author's Note: The Gayatri is a complete practice because it aligns the individual chakras of the subtle body with the corresponding luminous spheres of the cosmos. Through the sound vibration, we connect with our creator at the crown chakra illuminating the enlightened mind, a concept much greater than what we regularly think of as mind.

23. Ashley-Farrand, *Teacher of Mantra*, 293.

Appendix A

BUDDHISM

Breath Practices

Traditional Practice of Watching the Breath

Begin by selecting a quiet time and a place for your practice. Sit in a comfortable position with your spine erect yet relaxed. Allow your eyes to gently close and just begin to notice your breathing. Notice the rise and fall of your chest. Just notice. Invite yourself to use this simple watching of your breath to bring you into a spacious presence with your body and with the present moment. Begin to notice the sensations in your body. Again, just notice. Then notice what feelings and thoughts might be arising.

As sensations, feelings, and thoughts become present, invite yourself to put them onto a boxcar or onto a cloud and just imagine them moving past and away. Then return to simply watching the breath moving in and out of your body. This is your life-breath, your connection to your creator. It's how we know we live in a body and, when the breath ceases, it's how we know we have left our bodies. In between, we could say *we are breathed*. Allow yourself to fall into the rhythm of this sacred life force, your breath, this moment.

Each time some sensation, feeling, or thought arises and carries you away from this simple watching of your breath, place each onto the boxcar or cloud and just return again. And again. And again. The mind loves the past and future but doesn't have a lot of experience being in the present moment. It needs some training. But, as well-known Buddhist practitioner Jack Kornfield reminds us, it is best to be with this process much like we would be with a puppy we're training.[24] We don't need to beat or shame the puppy. We simply need to bring it back to the paper. Let's practice having a similar patience and compassion with ourselves.

You'll notice that each sitting brings new awareness. Sometimes you'll be able to return to the breath easily. Other times, it may be sensations, feelings, or thoughts that dominate. No matter. It's all good practice, for it's just how life is off the mat. Return again and again. And, over time, you will find yourself less caught by the comings and goings as you walk through your daily life.

If you're a beginner, I'd recommend starting with ten minutes and gradually building up to thirty minutes. At first, it may not appear that any benefit is arising from your practice. Trust that you are, indeed, cultivating a new way of being and that, in time, you'll begin to simply experience this new way of being *becoming you*.

Author's Note: The above is a composite from writings I've used to teach meditation over the years. I start here as nothing is needed but what is already available, our breath. It is so simple, yet not always easy. It is, graciously, truly our connection to the one who breaths us.

The Practice of Metta or Loving-Kindness (1,2,5)

The practice of *metta* or *loving-kindness* is an ancient practice that evokes feelings of loving-kindness toward our self and others. Know that cultivating such kindness is a process that can, in the beginning, bring up the opposite feelings. You may feel you're being disingenuous or mechanical. If this happens, know that you're actually being provided with a wonderful opportunity to *practice* extending such loving-kindness to yourself and to know that in its own time, even as you face your own resistance, loving-kindness will develop.

To begin the practice, sit in a relaxed and comfortable fashion. You may want to spend a little time with the

---

24. Kornfield, *Path with Heart*, 59.

Appendix A

Traditional Practice of Watching the Breath above to help center yourself. When you feel ready, begin to recite inwardly the following phrases to yourself. We begin with ourselves, as we know it is difficult to truly love others without loving ourselves first.

May I be filled with loving-kindness.
May I be well.
May I be peaceful and at ease.
May I be happy.

Repeat the phrases again and again, letting the words fill your being. Practice every day for at least a few weeks until you sense loving-kindness for yourself growing. The importance of cultivating this inner sense of self-love, kindness, and well-being cannot be underestimated. It's the foundation of all further practice we extend to others. It's like we fill ourselves up first so we can then have a deep inner well from which to draw. We also discover that, as we begin to expand self-acceptance and compassion to *all* parts of our self, we can, more easily, offer such compassion to others as well.

When you feel ready, in the same meditation period, choose to extend this blessing to someone you care for. Picture them in your mind's eye and recite the blessing to them. Over time, continue to extend out the blessing of *metta* to others: family members, friends, neighbors, others you may routinely see in your daily activities, all people everywhere. Then you can practice sending *metta* to someone with whom you have had, or are having, difficulty. This is an especially beautiful practice that can also bring challenges. But I have found that the greater the challenge, the more freedom awaits.

This is a wonderful practice that you can also take off your mat and into your life. Imagine silently sending *metta* to the one checking out your groceries, the postal clerk standing behind the counter, the one handing you your food in the drive-through. What happens, of course, is that this practice of extending *metta* to all beings changes us. We don't ask anymore that others or the

Sample Mantra Prayers from Six Faith Traditions

world be different. Instead, we ask that we be different and, so, our world becomes different.

Author's Note: The above is a composite from writings I've used to teach metta over the years. I find it the most profound practice not only for cultivating healthy self-love but also for practicing seeing with new eyes, experiencing and extending forgiveness, and releasing those ties that bind.

Om Mani Padme Hung (1,2,5)

Om—universal creative sound
Mani—jewel; the compassion in the heart for all beings
Padme—lotus flower; the wisdom that draws up through itself the muck from which it grows
Hung—(Tibetan pronunciation) throat chakra
Repeat 108+ times.

Source: Multiple—this is, perhaps, the most well-known mantra chanted in Buddhism.

Author's Note: This mantra represents a core teaching in my work and writings: like the lotus, we blossom, not in spite of, but because of. This mantra and teaching sets us free from any sense of victimhood and opens us to the gifts of all experience.

Gatae Gatae Paragatae Parasamgatae Bodhi Svaha (1,2,3,4,5)

Gatae—going
Paragatae—going further
Parasamgatae—gone
Bodhi Svaha—to full enlightenment
Repeat 108+ times.

This mantra is the final part of the *Heart Sutra*, thought by many to be the most powerful of Buddhist mantra practices. A central Buddhist scripture on heart awakening and obtaining enlightenment, the *Heart Sutra* teaches, "Form is emptiness, and emptiness is form," pointing to the root of all suffering—attachment to the illusion of life's permanence. Through dedicated spiritual practice, the attachments of the mind can be realized and released, but then there's still one final step to the full embodiment of Buddhahood—action. When you attain

Appendix A

unexcelled perfect enlightenment, you must attain the *function* of this enlightenment in the world. This is how we go, and continue going further, together, toward full enlightenment.

Source: *The Heart Sutra Commentary by Zen Master Seung Sahn*[25]

Author's Note: This is a beautiful practice that reminds us that we must walk the walk as our function in the world. We must live and make manifest, through our actions, our enlightenment in order to become the full embodiment of the Buddha.

Om Tarae Tuttarae Tuae Svaha (1,3,5)

Om—universal creative sound
Tarae—salvation from mundane dangers and suffering
Tuttarae—deliverance into the spiritual path conceived in terms of individual salvation, which leads to individual liberation from suffering
Turae—the culmination of the spiritual path in terms of deliverance into the altruistic path of universal salvation—the Bodhisattva path. In the Bodhisattva path, we aspire toward personal enlightenment, but we also connect compassionately with the sufferings of others and strive to liberate them at the same time as we seek enlightenment for ourselves.
Svaha—salutation
Repeat 108+ times.

Source: Bodhipaksa, "Green Tara Mantra."[26] In addition, the Foundation Dances and Walks: Dances of Universal Peace Manual (see Sufi section above for obtaining more information) asserts that Tara is so highly regarded that she is said to be the Mother of all Buddhas. She is known to the Tibetans as *The Faithful One* and *The Fierce Protectress*.

Author's Note: This practice reminds us that we go together. We have been given to one another. We belong to one another. Our individual enlightenment both affects and supports the enlightenment of all.

---

25. Billings, "Heart Sutra," paras. 1–11.
26. Bodhipaksa, "Green Tara Mantra," paras. 1–9.

SIKHISM

Breath Practices

Note: The breath and mantra practices offered here I learned in my many years of practicing and teaching Kundalini yoga.

Calm Heart Meditation

Sit in a relaxed pose. Place your left hand over your heart with fingers pointing straight across your chest. Bend your right arm as if you were going to take an oath. Place your fingers in *Gian Mudra*—tips of index finger and thumb touching with remaining fingers pointing upward. Relax both elbows. Close your eyes or look straight forward.

Inhale through your nose and suspend gently as long as comfortable.
Exhale through your nose and hold the breath out as long as comfortable.
This meditation creates a still point for the *prana* at the heart center.
Practice 3–11 minutes.

Source: Kundalini Yoga: Unlock Your Inner Potential through Life-Changing Exercise[27]

Author's Note: If you cannot do at least three full repetitions without having to take a normal breath, you are probably suspending and/or holding the breath out too long. The breath is to be relaxed and calming. It's an easy and very effective breath practice for beginners as well as for those more experienced.

27. Khalsa, *Kundalini Yoga*, 169.

Appendix A

Sitali Breath

Sit in a comfortable meditative posture with the spine straight. Curl the sides of the tongue upward and protrude it slightly past the lips.

Inhale deeply and smoothly through the tongue and mouth.
Then close the mouth and exhale through the nose.
Continue for as long as five minutes at a time.
To end, inhale and suspend the breath gently. Exhale and relax.
Sitali Breath is a cooling breath good for lowering fever and cooling anger. It rejuvenates and detoxifies when practiced regularly. Often the tongue tastes bitter at first. This is a sign of detoxification. As you continue the practice, the taste of the tongue will eventually become sweet.

Source: *Kundalini Yoga: Unlock Your Inner Potential through Life-Changing Exercise*[28]

Author's Note: It is thought to be genetic as to whether or not you're able to curl your tongue upward on both sides. If you're not able to do so, simply extend the tongue out as you're able. The same benefits await. This is great breath for cleansing and rejuvenating on all levels.

Mantra Prayers

Note: Because the Sikh mantra are often put to music, there are many quite beautiful musical versions for each of the mantras below. I would encourage you to seek out samples online.

Ek Ong Kar Sat Nam Siri Wahe Guru (1,2,3,4,5)

Ek Ong Kar—Creator/Creation
Sat Nam—Truth
Siri Wahe—great and beyond all description is divine wisdom
Guru—inner teacher

---

28. Khalsa, *Kundalini Yoga*, 26.

Sample Mantra Prayers from Six Faith Traditions

This mantra is referred to as the "Morning Call" and is best to do in the early hours of the morning. The eight parts are said to correspond to the body's eight energy centers, seven chakras plus the aura connecting you directly with your creator.

Practice 11–31 minutes

Source: Kundalini Yoga: Unlock Your Inner Potential through Life-Changing Exercise[29]

Author's Note: This is a complete practice one might call the Sikh Gayatri.

The Miracle Mantra: Guru Guru Wahe Guru Guru Ram Das (1,4,5)

Guru Guru—inner personal wisdom
Wahe—expanding that personal wisdom into the experience of the Infinite
Guru Guru—same personal wisdom
Ram—infinite manifesting power
Das—coming into your life as service
Special instructions for chanting:
Chant 5 repetitions on one breath.
1st repetition—begins with *Guru Guru*
2nd–4th repetitions—begin with *Guru Guru Guru*
Additional *Guru* repeated only at the end of the 5th repetition
Practice for 11–31 minutes

This mantra is known as the *miracle mantra* in honor of the fourth Sikh guru, Ram Das. According to Gurucharan Singh Khalsa, repeating this mantra five times connects us with the five elements of manifestation and takes us in a circular fashion from the personal to the infinite and back to the personal again. Chanting it allows us to clear away all the clouds to more fully realize prosperity and the fulfillment of our purpose in this lifetime. It provides the connections, attracts the situations, and brings the challenges we need to grow into our full radiance.

Source: Gurucharan Singh Khalsa, Ph.D., Kundalini Yoga Teacher Training. For more information, contact https://gurucharan.com/.

---

29. Khalsa, *Kundalini Yoga*, 174.

Appendix A

Author's Note: Practice of this mantra does, in fact, open us to the miracle of life in each moment and the infinite possibilities born of faith. Because it also incorporates a powerful breath practice, it truly does "clear away all the clouds," enabling us to more fully realize true fulfillment and joy.

Ra Ma Da Sa—Sa Say So Hung (1)

Ra—sun
Ma—moon
Da—earth
Sa—infinity
Sa Say—personal embodiment
So Hung—"I am Thou"
This is a mantra well known for its healing properties. Practice 11–31 minutes.

Source: *Kundalini Yoga: Unlock Your Inner Potential through Life-Changing Exercise*[30]

Author's Note: This is one of the most powerful healing practices I have been blessed to witness.

Kal Akal (3)

Kal—death
Akal—no death
Siri Kal—great death
Maha Akal—no great death
Akal Moorat—deathlessness
This is a protective mantra and is said to be able to remove the very shadow of death.
Repeat 11–31 minutes.

Source: Gurucharan Singh Khalsa, Ph.D., Kundalini Yoga Teacher Training. For more information, contact https://gurucharan.com/.

Author's Note: This is a mantra that is capable of capturing your heart completely. There is no doubt it dispels all negativity and leaves one in complete bliss.

Sa Ta Na Ma (4)

Sa—universe, totality
Ta—life, creation

---

30. Khalsa, *Kundalini Yoga*, 166.

Sample Mantra Prayers from Six Faith Traditions

Ma—rebirth, regeneration
Sa Ta Na Ma is referred to as the Kirtan Kriya. Kirtan means "divine song."
This mantra helps to clear the mind of unhelpful unconscious thoughts.
Practice 11—31 minutes.

Source: *Kundalini Yoga: Unlock Your Inner Potential through Life-Changing Exercise*[31]

Author's Note: I have found this mantra helps to stay focused on the unchanging "truth" beyond the changes inherent in rebirth and regeneration. This can be particularly helpful when we are going through a difficult or challenging transition.

Gobinday Mukanday (3)

Gobinday—sustaining
Mukanday—liberating
Udaaray—enlightening
Apaaray—infinite
Hareeung—destroying
Kareeung—creating
Nirnaamay—nameless
Akaamay—desireless
Chanting this mantra can eliminate karmic blocks or errors of the past. It balances the hemispheres of the brain, bringing compassion and patience.
Practice 11–31 minutes.

Source: Gurucharan Singh Khalsa, Ph.D., *Kundalini Yoga Teacher Training*. For more information, contact https://gurucharan.com/.

Author's Note: This mantra is well-known for its ability to cultivate courage, strength, and power.

Many of the Sikh mantras can be practiced as walking meditations. To learn more, explore *Breathwalk* at https://gurucharan.com/.

---

31. Khalsa, *Kundalini Yoga*, 160–61.

APPENDIX B

Stories from Lovers Who Have Braved the Wilderness

JAN'S STORY

Mantra operates somewhat like salve on a tender and/or agitated mind. When our energetics are out of kilter and our minds tend to want to take our discerning thoughts hostage, mantra can offer relief. Following participation in Reverend Dr. Rutt's Sanskrit Mantra course and sitting through several forty-day *Sadhanas* over the years, my mind became accustomed to resting in the energetics of certain sacred phrases. When my body gave me signs that my mind was about to run away with me, I would apply the remedy of a mantra.

Sometimes the results were startling.

At one point in her life, my daughter made the clear decision to make her way to Ghana in Africa. This was made possible by her clarity and a particularly affordable flight. We pounced on the opportunity, calling the airline to secure the flight. Unfortunately, the agent said that that flight and price were no longer available. That offer was off the table. I began to feel my stomach sinking. The agent could sense this and I asked if there was another flight that my daughter might fly out on. She said she would check. I was placed on hold, my mind poised to respond in agitation to my body's disappointment and mounting anxiety.

Instead, while placed on hold for a lengthy time, I chose to focus on the possibility of another affordable flight, even if on a less than ideal travel day. To soothe my unraveling self while waiting, I used the *Ganapatayee* mantra: "to remove obstacles to your goal."

Om Gam Ganapatayee Namaha, Om Gam Ganapatayee Namaha, Om Gam Ganapatayee Namaha, etc., salutations to *Ganesha* for overcoming obstacles!

"I'm sorry, there's nothing available. Could she fly on yet another day?"

Om Gam, Gam, Gam, Gam, Gam, Gam, Gam, Gam being the seed sound for obstacle removal. I repeated this quietly to myself as the agent placed me back on hold.

"Oh!" The agent's voice burst back on the phone. She was baffled, "I don't understand how this happened but the original flight at the original price just popped back up!" We accepted it immediately with delight—before rational thoughts might make it disappear once again!

But the story continues; complications arose around receiving the visa from New York. I was beginning to feel that the trip might not be in the cards. There was that frustrated sinking feeling again. I could feel myself beginning to rev up. Deep breath! *Om Gam, Gam, Gam, Gam, Gam, Om Gam Ganapatayee Namaha . . . !* I am hearing the woman say, "The visa office is closed now and the gentleman who was processing the paperwork left early for the holiday and you won't receive your travel papers in time. The office is closed on Monday. Sorry, nothing I can do!"

As I was preparing to find a way to break the news to my daughter I headed out through the garage to my car. Soon after hanging up the phone and following that emphatic "Sorry!" I saw there placed on the steps was the package containing the visa! We still have no idea how or when it got there!

I offered my gratitude to *Ganesha*, and to the Mystery, and was able to wish my daughter "bon voyage!" She had a safe and successful trip.

—Jan Grossman

Appendix B

PEGGY'S STORY

I began to practice the Lord's Prayer in Aramaic in May of 2013. Having had a spiritual experience, I felt drawn to this as a necessary response to help me understand and dedicate myself to my newfound life. Raised as a Catholic, I was familiar with the Lord's Prayer since the early 1960s. Yet, I was not drawn to recite it other than out of necessity during services.

After having heard the Lords' Prayer in Aramaic recited during a seminarian training class, my heart was stolen. I was captured by the beauty of it. Then I learned the more accurate translation of our Beloved's words ... and it all became so clear to me. How the ancient words permeated my being, reaching deep into my soul, as a long forgotten primal prayer. This prayer is with me each and every day now. I find myself calling out the words and basking in the light of our Beloved each time I do. The Aramaic Lord's Prayer reaches across the infinite life of my soul and carries me during times of weakness, and raises me above the ordinariness of my day and connects me to our Creator as no other prayer or action in my life has. I have been blessed by having this prayer as a part of my life and the experiences that have followed are, to say the least, gifts directly from our Beloved.

—Peggy Petahtegoose

CATE'S STORY

When I first began chanting mantra, I was at the lowest point of my life. I told a friend, "I have a death wish and I need a life wish." She said, "The only thing I know to tell you to do is chant *Nam Myoho Renge Kyo*." And I did. I was instructed to chant for my happiness. My teacher said, "If you cannot believe in your happiness, or that you deserve it or even that happiness is possible, chant then for the potential for your happiness." I was also told to treat the mantra like a scientific experiment, to see if it worked. To determine that, I was told to chant for something very specific—a material item, with a definite price, and all the details I cared to specify—the more the merrier. I was over 30k in debt at that time, living with two elderly parents who had to make a rapid move from their home of forty years because they'd lost their savings. I wrote and chanted and thought and doubted and chanted some more for what I wanted. Six months later, I drove a brand new cherry red Honda off the lot. I thought to my mantra, "Okay, you've got my attention."

I started to chant for everything I wanted, especially the impossible. I chanted for everyone, in the full assurance that my chanting was doing them good. I got most things for which I chanted, and when I didn't get them, I lost my wanting. My chanting became the opening to greater and greater possibilities.

When I chant mantra, I am transported by the vehicle of God. It is a fully visceral and embodied experience, with internal benefits like improved mood, patience, and hope. It's an energy raising, bliss building, peace realizing, utterly enlivening relaxation practice. The more I chant, the more devoted I am to chanting. Mantra brings gifts as the doorway to smashing skepticism. It provides me with joy and solace, humbling, and makes me eternally grateful. I am devoted to chanting because it makes me a vehicle, a vessel, a channel, a lamp, a ladder, a life boat for bringing the divine into our world. It affords me the means to return my blessings and joy to others.

If ever I were to choose a Sanskrit name, it will be Mantra.

—CATE SEMENTA

SHARON'S STORY

In my thirties, I experienced panic attacks, especially while driving on the highway in heavy traffic. What kept me going and got me through was *Aad Gurey Namay, Jugaad Gurey Namay, Sat Gurey Namay, Siri Guru Deva Namay*. I would chant it over and over again until I got through whatever rough patch was there, and I still use it to this day when I feel uncomfortable about anything. Spiritual grace to all who use this chant. *Sat Nam.*

—SHARON DENSMORE

Appendix B

DEB-ELLEN'S STORY

I began my practice with the chanting of *Ya Ahad, Ya Samad*. Not having any experience outside of Gregorian or *Taize* chant, I have sort of been crafting my chant from my daily experiences. In the first few months, I seemed to really be reciting these names of the Most Holy One while using prayer beads. Then, over the past four months, becoming more focused and centered, I have found myself refining my practice. I have added a very simple melody to my chant and, somehow, I have incorporated a process similar to leavening where I am rocking back and forth with most of my physical body in tune with my chant and vice versa. By involving more of my body, I feel not just my voice is tapping into the Universal Rhythm or Vibration but my whole being is entering into the Divine Voice or Dance. This chanting experience for me seems to both awaken me and, at the same time, draw me more deeply into a Centered Presence.

—Deb-Ellen Brown

SUE'S STORY

Learning the twenty-third Psalm in Hebrew has changed my life. I now say it every morning as part of my daily meditation. God as my Shepherd has given me a closer relationship with God. Walking through the Valley of the Shadow of Death with God has brought me comfort in difficult times. Saying the Psalm in Hebrew has opened my understanding of the passages. I feel I am closer to living God's will through making this Psalm a part of my daily life.

—Sue Hills

BONNIE'S STORY

I was studying the Lord's Prayer in Aramaic and had been listening to the CD and reciting the words in Aramaic for a few weeks. On a day that we were to meet together for class, I was reciting the prayer for an hour while driving. Once in class, we were reciting it together when it became evident that a powerful mystical energy was present. As I looked up, I witnessed an unmistakable vision and these words began to flow from me . . .

> *I saw God's face in the window*
> *It startled me*
> *So I looked away*
> *Rock-a-bye*
> *I saw God's face in the window*
> *It stirred something deep*
> *Slowly I looked away*
> *Rock-a-bye*
> *I saw God's face in the window*
> *My heart skipped a beat*
> *I could not look away*
> *Rock-a-bye*
> *I saw God's face in the window*
> *I thought it was me*
> *And I knew I was free*
> *Rock-a-bye*
> *Rock-a-bye*

—Bonnie McKellar

JOHN'S STORY

Eleven years ago, I had coronary artery bypass surgery. Just after starting out on one of my regular runs, I noticed how quickly winded I became. Because it had happened a couple of times before, I decided to get it checked out at the emergency room. "No big deal," I told myself. Of course, the ER doctor thought otherwise, wouldn't let me go home, and insisted I needed to be "transported" to the hospital, as in an "ambulance." At the hospital I flunked a stress test and an angiogram showed 80 percent blockage in my left main artery. Two days later I was operated on. So much for "no big deal."

People are placed in our lives for a reason. I guess I've always believed this but never took the time to reflect on it. A few years before, I found a yoga teacher named Stephanie and signed up for a class because that's what you do when you're working your way through a midlife crisis. And then I decided to take a course on spiritual development from Stephanie because I thought she was on the right path (whatever that was) and wanted some of that for myself. And then life happened, as in the coronary artery bypass, and I found myself sitting on a lawn chair during the first meeting of the spiritual development class because I couldn't yet sit on the floor after surgery. Right about then I knew it was important to be there because things stopped happening *to me* and *I started happening*. So, when I was introduced to mantra as part of the class and realized I could get to peace and healing without thinking my way there, it was a revelation. The only thing I needed was me and intention.

The mantra Stephanie gave me was *Om Ram Ramaya Swaha*, to balance healing energy channels in the body. I said it faithfully for months and still repeat it from time to time. Almost immediately I noticed the effects bringing about a state of clarity and well-being. Later, during cardiac rehab, I noticed that I could actually bring about measurable cardiac changes in the body by repeating the mantra. My physical goal was to resume distance running and my doctor frequently told me that my artery bypass surgery should result in better performance than ever.

In cardiac rehab, I ran on a treadmill with my body wired up to measure heart rate and blood pressure, the numbers displayed on a computer screen above the treadmill and a nurse carefully observing everything. I had a target heart rate range that it was important not to exceed. After a while I noticed that I could actually reduce my heart rate and blood pressure if I repeated the mantra while running. At first the nurse asked what I was saying and I would simply respond with, "It's my mantra." Later, if she noticed my heart rate was too high, she would suggest I decrease the speed of the treadmill and I would tell her I could get my heart rate down with the mantra. So, I began repeating *Om Ram Ramaya Swaha* and she watched the numbers on the monitors slowly work their way down. The highlight of our teamwork was when I was going for my best time ever for three miles and she yelled, "I need about two minutes of mantra!"

—JOHN SILVA

Stories from Lovers Who Have Braved the Wilderness

CAMILLA'S STORY

In the second class of our first year of seminary in the Tree of Life Interfaith Seminary program at the Tree of Life School for Sacred Living, Rev. Dr. Stephanie invited us to establish a daily spiritual practice or *Sadhana*. I already meditated—fairly casually, on and off over the past thirty years or so. But Rev. Stephanie was looking for a little more commitment and structure. I was ready.

I read all the relevant pages in the *Path of Crow: Journey to Your Inner Treasure* handbook that Rev. Dr. Stephanie had written, and I also took her up on the invitation of a one-on-one meeting to discuss what I would be doing for my daily spiritual practice. I'd decided on a thirty-one-minute total time, as I had read this brings changes to the *pranic* body, and thirty-one minutes felt right for me.

The structure of our daily practice was to be (1) stating our intention, (2) a breath meditation, (3) a mantra meditation, (4) traditional sitting meditation or centering prayer, and (5) restating our intention. Rev. Dr. Stephanie wisely intuited and recommended for me a Sikh breath meditation for the release of subconscious fear, and she said that I could choose one of the mantra—chants from the few that she would sing to me. I hadn't ever heard any chants or mantra like these and was enjoying listening to them. Then she began to sing the mantra *Gobinday Mukanday*, and it literally brought tears to my eyes. My whole being was resonating with that mantra. I felt like she was singing to my soul.

On my way home, I went to an appointment to have our car serviced and, while waiting, I was able to download the MP3 of PREM with Snatam Kaur singing *Gobinday* onto my iPhone. I had *Gobinday* blasting on my car speakers all the way home with the most enormous smile on my face. I felt like I was beaming with love. The whole of this rendition of *Gobinday* is only eleven minutes but I couldn't believe how soul-nourishing it felt. When I got home, I researched the words, and their meaning, and started exploring other mantra and chants as well.

> *Gobinday*—sustaining
> *Mukanday*—liberating
> *Udaaray*—enlightening

Appendix B

Apaaray—infinite
Hareeung—destroying
Kareeung—creating
Nirnaamay—nameless
Akaamay—desireless

Rev. Stephanie opened up a whole new world of ways to nourish my soul with mantra and chants, and it's a world that I continue to enjoy exploring.

—Camilla Sanderson

ILONA'S STORY

As a hospice chaplain, several times it seemed appropriate to offer to say the Lord's Prayer in Aramaic to people I visited. My experience has been that, each time as I recite, they close their eyes and this sense of peace descends. The response has been "Beautiful" or a simple smile. These have been moments to hold in the heart.

—Ilona Kwiecien

JULIA'S STORY

I have something really *wonderful* to share with you. Earlier this week, the *Gayatri* mantra called out to me like a seductive siren—only She could lead me safely to shore.

For a month, I'd been sailing the rocky seas of mid-winter blues and fighting a beast of a sinus infection. I heeded the siren's call and downloaded the Thomas Ashley-Farrand (Namadeva Acharya) version of this particular mantra, laughing out loud when I first heard it. "Way too fast!" I thought. "Time for the Amazing Slow Downer"—this cool software I'd recently purchased to learn some tricky choral music.

I imported the "Mother of All Mantra" and began to study it. At 50 percent speed, I could barely keep up with Namadeva. Slowly, over an hour's time and laughing at every turn, I sped it up. Eighty percent speed was perfect. Looking for more (of course) I turned it up to 100 percent. More joy! I managed to do at least 108 repetitions during the whole session. The mantra *Gayatri* helped me follow an inner impulse . . . to lift myself up and out . . . and connected me to the Universe and my Beloved once more. AUMMMMMMMMMMMMMMMM!

—Julia Eddy

CAROL'S STORY

Mantra has been a part of my life for about twenty-three years now, though in the past few years I realized it has been a part of me *all my life*.

On the morning of my birthday I awoke to a very strange and surreal dream with a "calling to the waters," and not just any waters but the coldest of waters during the coldest months of the year. Although the dream was surreal and strange its specific underlying meaning through images visually spoke loud and clear! Following the dream, I found myself in every area I traveled that day surrounded by water. As it rained, I met some friends for lunch at a restaurant on the river . . . imagine my skepticism, hesitation, like really???

There was a particular mantra that also came to me before my birthday and upon some research of this mantra I learned of its connection to my dream. The mantra was *Narayan Shabad* and is one of the many different names for the divine and relates to the quality of water. While researching deeper it came to me that the translation of the mantra is, "The Name of the Immaculate Lord is the Ambrosial Water, chanting it with the tongue, sins are washed away." The word "sin" makes me cringe in an uncomfortable way. During a conversation with my mentor and teacher Rev. Dr. Stephanie Rutt, she shed some light on the word "sin." She explained that sometimes the word "sin" can, in fact, be meant to mean "imperfections" as opposed to my upbringing meaning of "wrong doings." I am grateful for this light she shed upon my one-sided thought of a term that I was brought up with. Our conditioning can certainly drown us in ignorance!

Appendix B

Following a 140+ days chanting this mantra, I entered the ocean during the coldest month (March 8, 2020) with its water temperature being between 36–39 degrees. This was certainly no plunge as I stayed in the water for up to five minutes. It is said that it only takes thirteen to fifteen minutes for hypothermia to set in when in ocean water at this temperature. I did not realize any profound experience right off and in fact it took months for this to settle within the depths of my soul's experience. As a matter of fact, it was not till very recently that I realized the profundity of this actual experience.

The waters are the purity, not essentially the purity of "myself" but the purity of the depth of my being, my love, the most absolute divine within. The coldest of temperature in the waters is the underlying fears that really have no existence but within that of my thoughts, my conditioning from my upbringing.

Mantra flows along (like water) with your energy like streams flowing into the vast sea of the divine. I could not imagine my life without mantra, for it has saved me countless of times from drowning...

Source of mantra: www.spiritvoyage.com Contact Ajeet Kaur or Prabhu Nam Kaur for more information.

—Carol Gaudreau

STEPHANIE'S STORY

I call this story "The Mother Teresa Rosary: The Next Chapter." It is the "Next Chapter" because the first "Mother Teresa Story" occurred many years ago and is told in my book *An Ordinary Life Transformed: Lessons for Everyone from the Bhagavad Gita*.[1]

On the morning of November 21, 2010, half an hour before I was to teach a day-long seminary class, I felt a strange sensation. I went to the bathroom and saw that I was bleeding. Being five-plus years post-menopausal, I knew this wasn't good. After making a quick run to the store, I walked back into the Tree of Life and looked at my tapestry of Mother Teresa. I remembered how she carried on,

---

1. Rutt, *Ordinary Life*, 153–54.

fully committed to her mission, regardless of what was happening in her life. I would do the same, and we went on to have a great day.

The next day I made an appointment with my doctor and went out for some errands. When I returned home, my husband told me there was a message on our answering machine from Dick the barber, my former landlord. Except to wave through the barbershop window, I hadn't seen Dick in about a year and a half. My husband got his hair cut once a month so we'd stayed connected that way. But he'd never called me before.

In the message, he said he and his wife had just returned from Chimayo and that he'd brought me something. (Chimayo is where I'd bought my first Mother Teresa rosary many years before—a rosary that I had "lost" and Dick had "found" that he always believed had healed his daughter before he was finally able to return it to me in a way neither of us could have foreseen—the first "Mother Teresa Story.") He asked that I stop into the barbershop sometime to pick it up. Then he said, "I love you. God bless you." Now, although we were certainly connected because of the former experience with the rosary, he'd never spoken to me in that way. I remember feeling struck—something important was happening.

Meanwhile, my doctor told me I needed to see a gynecologist to rule out uterine cancer, and a few days later I had an appointment for an ultrasound. The nurse practitioner said that I had a thickening of the uterine wall and a polyp. She didn't appear concerned about the polyp but said I need to return as soon as possible to see the gynecologist to have a biopsy of the uterine wall.

After my appointment, I went by the barbershop to see Dick. He handed me a special Mother Teresa rosary with hearts he'd brought back from Chimayo. I thanked him fiercely and turned to leave but then instinctively heard him say, "Don't worry. We've got you covered. We put you in." Chimayo is known for many healings, as the dirt on the floor of the chapel has a long history of curative powers. There are crutches on the walls, notes, etc. I knew, in that moment, I was in trouble and, also, that I was going to be okay—regardless of the outcome. And, of course, Dick could have had no way of knowing, consciously, what was going on with me.

Appendix B

The day after I saw the bleeding, I had started a special healing practice using an ancient Vedic mantra of Shiva, the *Maha Mrityunjaya Mantra* well-known for its healing properties:

> Om Haum Joom Saha
> Om Bhur Bhuvaha Swaha
> Om Trayum-bakam Yajamahe
> Sughan'dhim Pushti Vardanam
> Urvaru'kamiva Bandhanan
> Mrityor Mukshiya Mamritat
> Swaha Bhuvaha Bhur Om
> Saha Joom Haum Om

As I continued to practice the mantra, I held my new Mother Teresa rosary against my belly and thanked her, Jesus, and the energies of Shiva for bringing ease where there was any dis-ease. I fell asleep each night and awoke up each day chanting with my rosary on my belly. And I started playing a beautiful instrumental of "Amazing Grace" constantly as I just knew some grace was surely being played out in my life. And I started to feel very deeply—sweetly—that, although I certainly didn't want to be seriously ill, what I wanted most was what my God wanted for me and I started ending my prayers with, "I belong to you, I love you most, so, whatever you want for me is fine." This tender awareness would turn out to be the most blessed gift of this experience.

When I returned for the biopsy, I remembered feeling oddly calm. After the nurses prepped me, the gynecologist came in looking quite serious and focused. Then, as she looked more closely at the screen, her whole facial expression changed. She clearly looked relieved and said, "Okay, this is good. I'm happy and happy for you. When I looked at your ultrasound last week I was concerned and coming in here I thought this was not going to be good. But, now, your uterine wall looks thin and perfectly healthy. We should get the polyp out and we'll send it for a biopsy but it doesn't look like anything to be concerned about."

And, indeed, there was nothing to be concerned about. All was well. Amen.

—Stephanie Rutt

Bibliography

Andrews, Andy. *The Traveler's Gift: Seven Decisions That Determine Personal Success*. Nashville: Thomas Nelson, 2002.

Ashley-Farrand, Thomas. *Healing Mantras: Using Sound Affirmations for Personal Power, Creativity, and Healing*. New York: Ballantine, 1999.

———. *Teacher of Mantra Instruction Manual*. Portland, OR: Saraswati, 2007.

Augustine. *Confessions*. Translated by R. S. Pine-Coffin. New York: Penguin, 1961.

Barks, Coleman, and Michael Green, eds. *The Illuminated Prayer: The Five Times Prayer of the Sufis*. New York: Random House, 2000.

Beck, Guy L. *Sonic Theology: Hinduism and Sacred Sound*. Columbia: University of South Carolina Press, 1993.

Billings, Al. "The Heart Sutra Commentary by Zen Master Seung Sahn." July 4, 2011. https://openbuddha.com/2011/07/04/the-heart-sutra-commentary-by-zen-master-seung-sahn/.

Bodhipaksa, trans. "Green Tara Mantra." https://www.wildmind.org/mantras/figures/greentara.

Born, Max. *Einstein's Theory of Relativity*. New York: Dover, 1962.

Clark, Glenn. *The Man Who Talks with the Flowers: The Life Story of Dr. George Washington Carver*. Austin, MN: Macalester Park, 2007.

Coelho, Paulo. *The Alchemist*. New York: HarperCollins, 1994.

Davis, John, ed. *Helen Keller: Rebel Lives*. New York: Ocean, 2003.

Douglas-Klotz. *Prayers of the Cosmos: Meditations on the Aramaic Words of Jesus*. New York: HarperCollins, 1990.

———. *The Sufi Book of Life*. New York: Penguin, 2005.

Emerson, Ralph Waldo. "Natural History of the Intellect: The Last Lectures of Ralph Waldo Emerson." https://www.waldorflibrary.org/images/stories/articles/gabriel_emerson.pdf.

Errico, Rocco A. *Setting a Trap for God*. Unity Village, MI: Unity House, 1997.

Felton, C. J. *Peace Is an Inside Job*. Bloomington, IN: Balboa, 2014.

Fernao, Xabier K. *365 Buddha Quotes*. Independently published, 2019.

Gass, Robert, and Kathleen Brehony. *Chanting: Discovering Spirit in Sound*. New York: Broadway, 1999.

BIBLIOGRAPHY

"Genesis 1 Hebrew Transliterated Bible." https://biblehub.com/interlinear/transliterated/genesis/1.htm.

Ginsburgh, Yitzchak. "Chedvah Breathing Method." https://www.inner.org/homepage/chedvah-breathing-method.

Hull, Bradford K. "Tiny Taoist and Zen Stories and Personal Ramblings." 2006. http://www.webtapestries.com/brad/stories.html.

Hurnard, Hannah. *Hinds' Feet on High Places*. Wheaton: Tyndale, 1975.

Kabir. *The Bijak of Kabir*. Translated by Linda Hess and Shukdeo Singh. New York: Oxford University, 2002.

Khalsa, Shakta Kaur. *Kundalini Yoga: Unlock Your Inner Potential Through Life-Changing Exercise*. New York: Dorling Kindersley, 2001.

Kidd, Sue Monk. *The Dance of the Dissident Daughter: A Woman's Journey from Christian Tradition to the Sacred Feminine*. New York: HarperCollins, 1996.

Kornfield, Jack. *A Path with Heart*. New York: Bantam, 1993.

Manning, Brennan. *The Furious Longing for God*. Colorado Springs: David C. Cook, 2009.

McGinn, Bernard. *Meister Eckhart: The Essential Sermons, Commentaries, Treatises and Defense*. Classic Western Spirituality. Mahwah, NJ: Paulist, 1981.

———. *The Mystical Thought of Meister Eckhart: The Man from Whom God Hid Nothing*. New York: Crossroad, 2001.

Meyer, Wali Ali, et al. *Physicians of the Heart: A Sufi View of the Ninety-Nine Names of Allah*. San Francisco: Sufi Ruhaniat International, 2011.

Molloy, Jack. "The 23rd Psalm." www.shalom-peace.com/Psalm23.html.

Muhaiyaddeen, M. R. Bawa. *Dhikr: The Remembrance of God*. Philadelphia: Fellowship, 1999.

Munk, Michael L. *The Wisdom in the Hebrew Alphabet: The Sacred Letters as a Guide to Jewish Deed and Thought*. Brooklyn, NY: Mesorah, 2012.

Nin, Anais. *The Quotable Anais Nin: 365 Quotations*. San Antonio: Sky Blue, 2015.

Radhakrishnan, S., trans. *The Principal Upanisads*. Daryaganj, New Delhi: Indus HarperCollins, 1994.

Rosenstein, Joseph G., trans. *Siddur Eit Ratzon*. Highland Park, NJ: Shiviti, 2006.

Rutt, Stephanie. *An Ordinary Life Transformed: Lessons for Everyone from the Bhagavad Gita*. Brookline, NH: Hobblebush, 2006.

Saint Mark Catholic Church. "Other Art at Shrine." http://saint-mark.net/church/about/shrine-to-fra-angelico/other-art-at-shrine/.

Satchidananda, Sri Swami. *The Living Gita: The Complete Bhagavad Gita and Commentary*. New York: Henry Holt, 1988.

Scherman, Nosson, et al., eds. *Tehillim: The Book of Psalms with an Interlinear Translation*. Brooklyn, NY: Mesorah, 2013.

Spink, Kathryn. *Mother Teresa (Revised and Updated): An Authorized Biography*. New York: HarperCollins, 2011.

Bibliography

Teresa of Avila. *Interior Castle: St. Teresa of Avila*. Translated by E. Allison Peers. Mineola, NY: Dover, 2007.

Terry, Lindsay. "Story behind the Song: His Eye Is on the Sparrow." https://www.staugustine.com/article/20151029/LIFESTYLE/310299971.

Therese of Lisieux. *The Poetry of Saint Therese of Lisieux*. Translated by Donald Kinney. Washington, DC: ICS, 1996.

www.ingramcontent.com/pod-product-compliance
Lightning Source LLC
Chambersburg PA
CBHW070919160426
43193CB00011B/1525